CLASSICS IN

From Homer to Juvenal

CLASSICS IN TRANSLATION

From Homer to Juvenal

Peter Jones

Duckworth

First published in 1998 by
Gerald Duckworth & Co. Ltd.
61 Frith Street, London W1V 5TA
Tel: 0171 434 4242
Fax: 0171 434 4420
Email: duckworth-publishers.co.uk

A catalogue record for this book is available
from the British Library

ISBN 0 7156 2868 2

Printed and bound in Great Britain by
Redwood Books Ltd, Trowbridge

Contents

Preface

This little book owes its inspiration to Tim Rostron, deputy arts editor of *The Daily Telegraph*. In 1997 he commissioned a series of essays for the newspaper that used modern translations to introduce the work of twenty major Greek and Roman authors to the general reader. The original *Telegraph* essays are gathered here, most slightly expanded. None of them claims to do any more than reflect what excites me about the authors concerned.

If readers are inspired to buy the translations, excellent. If they are even more inspired to learn a little Latin and Greek, my twenty-part *Learn Latin* (Duckworth, 1997) and *Learn Ancient Greek* (Duckworth, 1998) – both also serialised in *The Daily Telegraph* – would make as good a place to start as any. If they need general introductions to the Greeks and Romans, I recommend The Joint Association of Classical Teachers' *The World of Athens* (Cambridge, 1984) and Peter Jones and Keith Sidwell, *The World of Rome* (Cambridge, 1997).

I am grateful to Clare, Isolde, Oliver and Sir Bruce Roxby for casting a shrewd eye over the whole book and improving it in many places.

September 1998   Peter Jones

Acknowledgements

Every effort has been made to contact all the publishers of translations quoted in this book, and we are grateful to all those who have given us permission to reprint. Full publication details are given in the text for each translation after the first extract quoted. Additional acknowledgments are as follows:

Early Greek Philosophy, tr. © Jonathan Barnes, 1987; *The Knights; Peace; The Birds; The Assembly Women; Wealth* by Aristophanes, tr. © David Barrett & Alan H. Sommerstein, 1977; *Letters from a Stoic: Epistulae Morales ad Lucilium* by Seneca, tr. © Robin Alexander Campbell, 1969; *The Wasps; The Poet and the Women; The Frogs* by Aristophanes, tr. © David Barrett, 1964; *Three Plays: Alcestis; Hippolytus; Iphigenia in Tauris* by Euripides, tr. © Philip Vellacott, 1953; *The Annals of Imperial Rome* by Tacitus, tr. © Michael Grant Publications Ltd. 1956, 1959, 1970, 1973, 1975, 1977, 1989; *The Sixteen Satires* by Juvenal, tr. © Peter Green, 1967, 1974; *The Erotic Poems* by Ovid, tr. © Peter Green, 1982; *Phaedrus & The Seventh and Eighth Letters* by Plato, tr. © Walter Hamilton, 1973; *The Iliad* by Homer, tr. © Martin Hammond, 1987; *Metamorphoses* by Ovid, tr. © Mary M. Innes, 1955; *On the Nature of the Universe* by Lucretius, tr. © R.E. Latham, 1951; *On Britain and Germany* by Tacitus, tr. © H. Mattingly, 1958; *The Iliad* by Homer, tr. © The Estate of E.V. Rieu, 1950; *The Odyssey* by Homer, tr. © The Estate of E.V. Rieu and D.C.H. Rieu, 1991; *The Laws* by Plato, tr. © Trevor J. Saunders, 1970; *The Histories* by Herodotus, tr. © The Estate of Aubrey de Selincourt, 1954, and A.R. Burn, 1972; *The Last Days of Socrates* by Plato, tr. © Hugh Tredennick, 1954, 1959, 1969; *The Bacchae and Other Plays* by Euripides, tr. © Philip Vellacott, 1954, 1972; *Orestes and Other Plays* by Euripides, tr. © Philip Vellacott, 1972; *Prometheus Bound; The Suppliants; Seven Against Thebes; The Persians* by Aeschylus, tr. © Philip Vellacott, 1961; *The Peloponnesian War* by Thucydides, tr. © Rex Warner, 1954; *Thyestes; Phaedra; The Trojan Women; Oedipus with Octavia* by Seneca, tr. © E.F. Watling, 1966; *The Pot of Gold; The Prisoners; The Brothers Menaechmus; the Swaggering Soldier; Pseudolus* by Plautus, tr. © E.F. Watling, 1947; *The Histories* by

Acknowledgements

Tacitus, tr. © Kenneth Wellesley, 1964, 1972; *Aeneid* by Virgil, tr. © David West, 1990; *The Poems of Catullus*, tr. by Peter Whigham, © Penguin Books Ltd., 1966; *The Georgics* by Virgil, tr. © L.P. Wilkinson, 1982; all reproduced by permission of Penguin Books Ltd. *The Eclogues* by Virgil, tr. © Guy Lee, 1984, reprinted by permission of Guy Lee.

Epigrams of Martial English'd by Divers Hands, © The Regents of the University of California, 1987.

Ted Hughes, *Tales from Ovid*, 1997, reprinted by permission of Faber & Faber, and Farrar, Straus & Giroux; Ted Hughes, *Seneca's Oedipus*, 1969, reprinted by permission of Faber & Faber.

The Histories by Herodotus, A Norton Critical Edition, tr. Walter Blanco, © 1992 by W.W. Norton & Co. Inc.; *The Odyssey*: A New Verse Translation, tr. © Albert Cook, 1967; both reprinted by permission of W.W. Norton & Co. Inc.

'Agamemnon' from *The Oresteia* by Aeschylus, tr. © Robert Fagles, 1966, 1967, 1975; *The Iliad* by Homer, tr. © Robert Fagles, 1990; 'Antigone' from *Three Theban Plays* by Sophocles, tr. © Robert Fagles, 1982; *The Odyssey* by Homer, tr. © Robert Fagles, 1966; all reprinted by permission of Viking Penguin, a division of Penguin Putnam Inc.

Josephine Balmer, *Sappho*, 1984, reprinted by permission of Bloodaxe Books.

C. Day-Lewis, *The Aeneid of Virgil*, 1995, reprinted by permission of Peters Fraser & Dunlop.

Martin West, *Greek Lyric Poetry*, 1993; H.D.F. Kitto, *Sophocles*, 1994; R. Waterfield, *Herodotus: The Histories*, 1998; James Morwood, *Euripides: Helen*, 1997; Stephen Halliwell, *Aristophanes: Lysistrata*, 1997; R. Waterfield, *Plato: Republic*, 1993; E. Segal, *Plautus: Four Comedies*, 1996; Sir Ronald Melville, *Lucretius: On the Nature of the Universe*, 1998; Guy Lee, *The Poems of Catullus*, 1990; A.D. Melville, *Ovid's Metamorphoses*, 1986; D.S. Levene, *Tacitus: The Histories*, 1997; Niall Rudd, *Juvenal: The Satires*, 1991; all reprinted by permission of Oxford University Press.

Peter Green, *Ovid: The Poems of Exile*, 1994, reprinted by permission of David Higham & Associates Ltd.

Allen Mandelbaum, *The Aeneid of Virgil*, 1981; *Homer: The Odyssey*, 1990; Robert Fitzgerald, *Homer: The Iliad*; all reprinted by permission of Bantam Books Inc.

Fleur Adcock and Peter Porter's tanslations from *The Greek Anthology* are reprinted by permission of the respective authors.

Introduction

When the Roman poet Catullus talks of the way his mistress Lesbia has deserted him, he imagines a flower on the edge of a meadow clipped by a passing plough. When his love turns to hatred, in a crudely horrible expression he imagines Lesbia in the back-alleys and doorways of Rome 'tossing off (literally 'peeling the skin off') the great-hearted sons of Remus'.

These sentiments were composed around 60 BC. They are over 2,000 years old. But there is nothing difficult or complicated, let alone élitist, about them. We recognise what Catullus is trying to do when he idealises his innocence on the one hand, and humiliates Lesbia on the other. We acknowledge that we too have felt and responded like this. These are feelings universal to mankind.

Greek and Latin have been called dead languages. But these snippets, like the works of almost all the great ancient authors, show that there is nothing dead about them. Or if they are, Shakespeare and Dickens are equally dead. What they are, of course, is immortal.

Greek and Roman literature is certainly *different*, however, and this is where the fascination lies. For these are the first literate cultures of the Western world and therefore the first voices that speak to us in the Western world. But they are voices untouched by Christianity, by the industrial and mass communications revolution, by any scientific understanding of how the mind and body work, let alone the universe. Greeks and Romans believed in a multiplicity of gods, invisible powers or forces (frequently personalised by poets) that, rather like gravity, required no belief or love, but only acknowledgement (walk along any cliff top, say how much you love and believe in gravity, and step off. You'll get the point).

Yet it is to these two peoples that we still look back in awe. The reason is that, for all their difference and distance, we see them beginning to articulate with diamond-brilliant clarity the ideas, feelings and

1

problems we still have to deal with today, and not a cliché in sight. Western civilisation begins with them. The terms of the debate have hardly changed.

The Greek philosopher Socrates, for example, points out that we know what the purpose of a shoe is, what a good shoe is, and where we can buy one. So what is the purpose of man, what makes a good man, and where can we find one? And what do you mean by 'good'? 'Good' in itself, or 'good' *at* something?

Tragic poets like Sophocles turn to myth. In *Antigone*, King Creon refuses his nephew Polyneices burial. Polyneices' sister Antigone determines to bury him, whatever the penalty. Here are age-old conflicts – a split family, youth against age, the state against the individual, women against men, men against the gods.

The Latin poet Lucretius is convinced that it is fear of death that destroys men's lives. His brilliant poem *On the Nature of the Universe* sets out to banish that fear by arguing the gods have no interest in us and that anyway we are nothing but atoms which, at death, disappear into the great atom pool. Modern traumas about death and loss would have disgusted him. He must have thought he had silenced these bogeys for ever.

In the original Latin and Greek, these great works and all the others we shall be looking at stand comparison with the finest literature anywhere in the world. Quality will out. This is why they have been read down the millennia. The interesting thing, however, is that, at a time when the languages are having a tough time of it in schools, the number of people that are turning to read the ancient classics is growing fast.

What has happened is that people are now able to get their hands on ancient literature in a form they can understand – in English, and in good, strong, everyday English too. It is largely down to the dramatic growth of the popular translation industry over the past ten years that this has come about (going back originally to E.V. Rieu's invention of it in 1946 with Homer's *Odyssey*, the first ever Penguin translation). The classics have been democratised – and not before time. As the cultural history of the medieval ages and renaissance shows, revivals in the classics are always driven by the emergence of translations.

The result is that when a new translation of Homer's *Iliad* or *Odyssey* comes out by a well-known translator like the American Robert Fagles, it hits the headlines. When media moguls observe the impact of such a translation, they begin to sense a market, and soon stage, screen and television are reinterpreting the classics for today's market, and that feeds the classics back again to yet wider audiences.

Since the classics are for all time, they do not let you down. I am sure that no one who has seen the film *The English Patient* and then bought a copy of Herodotus has been disappointed with his hilarious stories about how to catch crocodiles and nick gold from jealous gold-digging ants, or his terrifying accounts of men who in their pride crossed the gods and paid for it.

This revival – renaissance, almost – is an exciting prospect for those unacquainted with ancient literature. It opens up new worlds of under-standing, and self-understanding too. It stretches our capacity to sympathise with and come to terms with a very different world. It puts us in contact with thousands of years of human experience. As there is an ecology of the environment, concerned with saving the natural world for the future generations to enjoy, so there is an ecology of culture. In reading two fine ancient literatures we do our bit to transmit the great achievements of the past to those yet unborn. Finally, and perhaps most stimulating of all, we can enjoy the points of comparison: here is the Roman satirist Juvenal (AD 100) – how good is *Private Eye*?

There are, of course, good and bad translations. Those of us enjoying the incomparable blessing of being able to read Greek and Latin in the original will always find something to moan about. Imagine Shake-speare in Yoruba. Translations can go only so far. Yet if much is lost, much remains – if it is allowed to.

In this respect, the history of translation has a fascinating story to tell. The Loeb editions of Greek and Latin Classics, for example, – text on one side, translation on the other – tended in the past to leave passages of explicit sexual activity in the original language, merely repeating the Latin or Greek on the translation page. This, of course, is very helpful to schoolboys who can concentrate all their efforts on these bits without having to plough through the rest, and it polishes up their dictionary skills no end (it has been wittily said that you cannot make love if you do not know Latin and Greek, since so many of the names for the necessary parts and activities derive from the ancient languages).

The first Loeb edition of the Roman poet Martial took a different tack, translating the rude bits into Italian (Italians presumably being irredeemably corrupt already). But the publishers still could not bring themselves to print the Italian *cunno* and printed *c---o* instead. Phew! The morals of a nation saved again.

Nineteenth-century translators faced even greater problems with Greek pederasty. The Victorian age regarded the ancient Greeks with an almost holy reverence, as touchstones of morality on a par with Christianity. So they were appalled to find the philosopher Plato advocating the physical love of boys as a crucial step on the path to ultimate Goodness. W.H. Thompson, Master of Trinity College, Cambridge, said 'it seems almost impossible that Plato can seriously have entertained the paradox that *paidôn erôs* ('physical love of boys') was a necessary step to moral perfection.'

Faced with this dilemma, one translator converted a passage in Plato's *Phaedrus* about the love of a man for a boy into the love of a man for a girl. This was all very well until Plato described how the 'girl' grew up and went off to find a wife. In despair, the translator omitted this passage.

Those days are past. We *want* the challenge of understanding what makes ancient cultures tick (even though modern translations will, in a hundred years time, be condemned as roundly for seeing the ancient world through *our* coloured spectacles). Probably the only things that shocks us nowadays is death, the most natural (and certainly inevitable) thing in the world. The Roman emperor Marcus Aurelius urged us to 'go to our rest with a good grace, as an olive falls in its season, with a blessing for the earth that bore it and a thanksgiving to the tree that gave it life'. The modern olive is, in my experience, less articulate, but it's the thought that counts. Greek and Roman authors were masters of the pithy, pointed, elegant one-liner.

But when one has spent much of one's life, as I have, reading ancient literature in the original, it does not surprise me that it has exerted such a powerful hold on the imagination of our ancestors.

The early Church, for example, acknowledged the power and efficiency of education in Latin and Greek, however pagan the world which that education dealt with. When the pagan gods really went over the top, the Church fathers solved the problem by turning them into allegories.

When educated young men in the First World War went to fight at Gallipoli, which lies opposite Troy, they imagined they were refighting the Trojan War and took their Homer with them. Patrick Shaw-Stewart called on Achilles to be with him in battle, remembering the moment in the *Iliad* when Achilles, a halo of fire round his head, drove the Trojans back with a terrifying shout from the trenches. Imbros is one of the islands from which attacks on Gallipoli were launched:

> I will go back this morning
> To Imbros over the sea;
> Stand in the trench, Achilles,
> Flame-capped, and shout for me.

When civil servants went out to administer the colonies, they saw themselves as Roman governors and took their Cicero to remind themselves how to do it. Cicero was an advocate, statesman and philosopher. He governed a province in Asia Minor (modern Turkey), gave lengthy and fascinating advice to his brother on how to do it, and prosecuted Verres, corrupt governor of Sicily.

So I can well understand why the Victorians judged Greek and Latin literature to be almost as powerful and valuable a force for good as the Bible, and why they were so disturbed when they found some ancient authors falling below the high moral standards set for them.

But in this little book we are not in the judging business – or rather, if we are, it is to answer only one question: are the Greek and Latin classics worth reading in translation, whatever their 'message'? I hope to show that the answer is overwhelmingly 'yes'. Time then to start thinking seriously about the ultimate experience – reading them in the original (see *Preface*).

Note

These little essays lack critical sophistication. For example, when Catullus talks about himself, I rather daringly take him at his word. This will shock those who believe he was inventing people and places to write poetry about. But I judged that agonising over theoretical issues had no place in a book like this. Those who like their criticism sado-masochistic will find no lack of it on the open shelves of otherwise reputable bookshops.

1

Homer: The *Iliad* .

Homer's *Iliad* is the first work of Western literature (*c.* 720 BC). Its subject is the Trojan War. This was fought between Greeks and Trojans because Trojan Paris stole Greek Helen and took her back to Troy. But this is of no interest to Homer (he hardly mentions it). The *Iliad*'s hero is Achilles (Greek Achilleus). It is an epic.

Think 'epic' and we think of great heroes like Charlton Heston in *El Cid*, or *Braveheart*. We think of clashes with destiny and the birth of nations. But see how the *Iliad* begins (Ilium is the town the Greeks are attacking, Troy the area). Homer first invokes the Muse, goddess of Memory:

> Sing, goddess, the anger of Achilleus, son of Peleus, the accursed anger which brought uncounted anguish on the Achaians [=*Greeks*] and hurled down to Hades many mighty souls of heroes, making their bodies the prey to dogs and the birds' feasting: and this was the working of Zeus' will.
> (Martin Hammond, *Homer: The Iliad*, Penguin, 1987)

What on earth is this? An *angry* hero? Angry at injustice, we expect. No: the anger is 'accursed'. It results in 'uncounted anguish' not for the enemy but for Achilles' own side, the Greeks. It leads to their deaths and leaves them unburied, carrion for dogs and dinner for the birds. And Zeus willed it!

This does not sound like Charlton Heston. What is Achilles doing destroying his own side? What is the Greek god Zeus on about? In fact, it hardly sounds like epic at all. The Greek polymath Aristotle four hundred years later saw it for what it was – tragedy. It is an unforgettable start for Western literature – not a chauvinistic, short-sighted, we-stuffed-Johnny-Foreigner, rant for Greeks against Trojans, but an exploration of the psychology of the greatest of Greek military heroes, the ferociously self-willed Achilles, whose fury will cause the death of many other Greeks but especially of his dearest companion Patroclus; doom Achilles himself to die young; and finally destroy Hector, the great Trojan leader (foreshadowing, but not actually describing, the destruction of Troy itself). Some epic.

Insulted by the Greek leader Agamemnon who had taken his girl Briseis, Achilles stalks out of the battle with his close companion Patroclus, confident that he will soon be welcomed back, honoured with sensational compensation. The goddess Athene has promised him this; and his divine mother Thetis has also wrung out of Zeus an agreement that the Trojans will start winning, thus forcing the Greeks to make a deal with Achilles. But when the compensation duly arrives, Achilles executes an astonishing *volte-face* and will have none of it, eventually promising to return to the fight only if the Trojans get as far as burning the Greek ships. Here are some extracts from his powerful rejection speech:

> Stay at home or fight your hardest – your share will be the same. Coward and hero are honoured alike. Death does not distinguish do-nothing and do-all ... Why is it that the Argives [*Greeks*] must fight the Trojans? Why did the son of Atreus [*Agamemnon, brother of Menelaus whose wife was Helen*] raise an army and sail here? Was it not because of lovely-haired Helen? Are the sons of Atreus the only ones of humankind to love their wives? ... I will not join him [*Agamemnon*] in plan or action. He has cheated me and wronged me. He will not work his cheating tongue on me again. Enough already. No, he can take himself to ruin at his own pace – Zeus the counsellor has robbed him of his wits. I abominate his gifts, I care not a splinter for the man.
> (Hammond)

This is the turning point of the *Iliad*. Achilles' decision, taken (as usual) with supreme confidence that he is right and everyone else wrong, will lead directly to Patroclus' and his own death. The Greeks are thrown back, Trojan Hector threatens to fire their ships and Patroclus (cunningly persuaded by the wise old Greek counsellor Nestor) persuades Achilles to send him (Patroclus) into battle, dressed in Achilles' armour. Achilles agrees. The moment is rich in tragic irony and pathos. Here Achilles prays to Zeus for Patroclus' safe return:

1. Homer: The Iliad

'Oh! Be his guard thy providential care,
Confirm his heart and string his arm for war:
Press'd by his single force, let *Hector* see
His Fame in Arms not owing all to me.
But when the fleets are saved from foes and fire,
Let him with conquest and renown retire;
Preserve his arms, preserve his social train,
And safe return him to these eyes again!'
Great Jove consents to half the chief's request
But heav'ns eternal doom denies the rest;
To free the fleet was granted to his prayer;
His safe return, the winds dispersed to air.
(Alexander Pope (1720), *The Iliad of Homer*, Penguin, 1996)

Patroclus charges into battle but, ignoring Achilles' warnings not to go too far, is killed by a combination of Apollo (who, in a scene of unmatched power and horror, knocks Achilles' impenetrable armour off his back) and the Trojan leader Hector. As Patroclus dies, he foresees Hector's death too:

'One more thing – take it to heart, I urge you –
you too, you won't live long yourself, I swear.
Already I see them looming up beside you – death
and the strong force of fate, to bring you down
at the hands of Aeacus' great royal son ... Achilles!'
Death cut him short. The end closed in on him.
Flying free of his limbs
his soul went winging down to the House of Death,
wailing his fate, leaving his manhood far behind,
his young and supple strength.
(Robert Fagles, *Homer: The Iliad*, Penguin, 1990)

Here is the moment when Achilles hears of Patroclus' death. He is talking to his mother, the goddess Thetis, who has responded to his scream of grief. It soon becomes clear that if he kills Hector, he dies next. Achilles is speaking:

'... the spirit within does not drive me
to go on living and be among men, except on condition

9

that Hector first be beaten down under my spear, lose his life
and pay the price for stripping Patroklos, son of Menoitios'.
Then in turn Thetis spoke to him, letting the tears fall:
'Then I must lose you soon, my child, by what you are saying,
since it is decreed your death must come soon after Hector's.'
Then deeply disturbed, Achilles of the swift feet answered her:
'I must die soon then; since I was not to stand by my companion
when he was killed.'
(Richmond Lattimore, *The Iliad of Homer*, Chicago, 1951)

And so Achilles, assuming responsibility for everything that has hap-
pened, returns to the fighting, not to win glory or restore national pride,
but with only one thought in mind – revenge on Hector for Patroclus'
death. Here is a true tragic hero: one who, far from being ignorant of
what fate has in store, willingly embraces it, even though it means his
death.

Hector is portrayed in a deeply sympathetic light – indeed, the
Trojans are never represented as an evil enemy, requiring annihilation
for the good of mankind. Scenes of life in Troy contrast strongly with
the Greek army camped out on the Trojan plain far from home, and
here Hector meets his wife Andromache and their young child Asty-
anax. Astyanax is frightened by his helmet:

As he finished [*speaking*], glorious Hector held out his arms to
take his boy. But the child shrank back with a cry to the bosom of
his girdled nurse, alarmed by his father's appearance. He was
frightened by the bronze of the helmet and the horsehair plume
that he saw nodding grimly down at him. His father and lady
mother had to laugh. But noble Hector quickly took his helmet
off and put the dazzling thing on the ground. Then he kissed his
son, dandled him in his arms, and prayed to Zeus and the other
gods: 'Zeus, and you other gods, grant that this boy of mine may
be, like me, pre-eminent in Troy; as strong and brave as I; a
mighty king of Ilium. May people say, when he comes back from
battle, "Here is a better man than his father." Let him bring home
the bloodstained armour of the enemy he has killed, and make his
mother happy'.

... As he spoke, glorious Hector picked up his helmet with its

horsehair plume, and his wife set out for home, shedding great tears and with many a backward look.
(E.V. Rieu, *Homer: The Iliad*, Penguin 1950)

The genius of Homer is well displayed in this passage. Notice in particular his reticence. The modern novelist at this point would deafen the reader with pages of rant about how sad/tragic/pathetic it all was and ooh isn't war horrible and poor Andromache and what about the baby and so on. Not Homer. He offers no interpretation of the characters' words and actions. He simply reports how they speak, act and react, and leaves us to respond. Consider that simple 'with many a backward look' (one word in Greek, *entropalizomenê*). This is a woman who will never see her man again, and knows it. All she can do is look back at him as he returns to battle. That single phrase captures the whole experience. No comment is required.

When Achilles finally traps Hector, he is still so deranged with grief and rage at Patroclus' death that he rejects Hector's pleas for ransom of his corpse so that it can be buried (the most basic of human rights):

'Beg no more, you fawning dog – begging me by my parents!
Would to god my rage, my fury would drive me now
to hack your flesh away and eat you raw –
such agonies you have caused me! Ransom?
No man alive could keep the dog-packs off you,
not if they haul in ten, twenty times that ransom
and pile it here before me and promise fortunes more –
no, not even if Dardan [*Trojan*] Priam [*Hector's father*] should
    offer to weigh out
your bulk in gold! Not even then will your noble mother
lay you on your deathbed, mourn the son she bore ...
The dogs and birds will rend you – blood and bone!'
(Fagles)

And so Hector dies, but (like Patroclus) with a fatal vision of his killer's impending doom:

'But now beware, or my curse will draw god's wrath
upon your head, that day when Paris and lord Apollo –
for all your fighting spirit – destroy you at the Scaean gates!'

Death cut him short. The end closed in around him.
Flying free of his limbs
his soul went winging down to the House of Death,
wailing his fate, leaving his manhood far behind,
his young and supple strength.
(Fagles)

But Achilles, who always goes to self-destructive extremes, has this time gone too far in refusing to allow Hector's body burial. The gods intervene to ensure that the body is returned, and Hector's father Priam, the aged king of Troy, is sent by the gods in secret to Achilles' tent. Risking everything, Priam 'kissed those hands, terrible, murderous, that had killed so many of his sons' and supplicates Achilles for the return of Hector's corpse. Pity prevails over blind fury and Hector is returned to Troy and buried. And so the *Iliad* ends – with Achilles' death and Troy's fall still to come. As Homer insists at the beginning, the *Iliad* is about Achilles and his wrath, not the fall of Troy, and that is now worked out.

The first glory of the *Iliad* is its character drawing. These heroes burst with vigour and life. The similes come next, over three hundred of them. The god Apollo destroys the wall round the Greek camp like a boy destroying a sandcastle on the beach; the Greek army roars like surf driven on shore by a south wind; a dead hero's head slumps 'as on the stalk a poppy falls, weighed down by showering spring'; weapons fly over a hero 'like flies in a sheepfold over brimming milk-pails' (ancient Mediterranean stomachs could not digest cow's milk). Here Patroclus comes in tears to report to Achilles that the Greeks are in serious trouble, and Achilles addresses him:

'... Patroclus,
why all the weeping? Like a small girl-child
who runs beside her mother and cries and cries
to be taken up, and catches at her gown,
and will not let go, looking up in tears
until she has her wish: that's how you seem'
(Robert Fitzgerald, *Homer: The Iliad*, World's Classics, 1974)

In the carnage of battle, the similes constantly evoke other worlds, especially the worlds of nature, the family and peace – worlds, surely,

12

of Homer's personal observation. The similes also increase the stature, dignity and value of human life by comparing it with the permanent, unchanging order of the natural world. For the record, Achilles is most likened to fire (fourteen times), a god (seven times) and a lion (five times); and his relationship with Patroclus is likened to a family relationship nine times (as in the above passage).

And then there are the gods. They take sides: Athene and Hera for the Greeks, Apollo and Poseidon for the Trojans, with Zeus trying to hold the ring. All-powerful, awesome and immortal, but otherwise all too human in their interests and behaviour and almost completely indifferent to human morality (they just want to be acknowledged as gods through prayer and ritual, especially sacrifice), they intervene shamelessly on behalf of their favourites. Since gods support only winners, their intervention confers tremendous status on humans. Here Apollo has realised that Hector is doomed and abandons him. That means Athene can now move in mercilessly on Achilles' behalf as he vainly chases Hector rounds the walls of Troy and address him:

'Illustrious Achilles, darling of Zeus, our chance has come to go back to the ships with a glorious victory for Achaean [*Greek*] arms. Hector will fight to the bitter end, but you and I are going to kill him. There is no escape for him now, however much the Archer-King Apollo may exert himself and grovel at the feet of his father, aegis-bearing Zeus. Stay still now and recover your breath, while I go to Hector and persuade him to fight you.' Achilles was well pleased and did as she told him.
(Rieu)

Note Achilles' delight. No hero was demeaned by divine support – quite the reverse.

Awesome as the gods can be in Homer's third-person descriptions of them (e.g. Poseidon setting out to sea in his chariot), nevertheless it is noticeable that when heroes *talk* about them or *react* to them, they do so in a remarkably independent spirit, with few intimations of fear or reverence. These heroes are not puppets, but self-willed individuals. So when Apollo thunders at the Greek hero Diomedes to step back, Diomedes does – but 'just a little'. When Athene promises that Achilles will be fully compensated for Agamemnon's insult, she asks him to pay attention, 'if you will obey me'!

There is no complex theology about these gods. Fate, as has been well said, is the will of the poet, and Homer the artist deploys gods for whatever strategic purpose he requires. In depicting the interaction between gods and humans, he sometimes plays the 'human free-will' card, sometimes the 'iron fate of the gods' card. There is no consistency here, but Homer is not a theologian. He is an epic poet, and the story is all.

The translations

The *Iliad* is oral poetry. It was recited, its 24 books taking over 30 hours to perform. It is full of digressions, lengthy speeches, battle scenes and repetitions. But this is the nature of oral poetry. One soon comes to enjoy its expansiveness and descriptiveness.

Hammond and Rieu are both prose translations, Hammond the more accurate and meatier, Rieu the easiest read of them all. Lattimore, Fagles and Fitzgerald, all Americans, attempt forms of blank verse. Of them, only Lattimore sticks closely to the Greek, usually with effect. Fagles and Fitzgerald are very popular. Alexander Pope's magnificent translation (1715-1720), with Pope's own notes and index, is a must for all who love poetry. George Steiner's *Homer in English* (Penguin, 1996) is a wide-ranging anthology of translations.

Newcomers to Homer should first read Books 1, 6, 9, 16, 18, 22 and 24. These are the kernel of the story.

2

Homer: The *Odyssey*

Homer's *Odyssey* is the second work of Western literature, *c*. 700 BC. Did the same man also compose the *Iliad* (*c*. 720 BC)? Ancient Greeks generally thought so. Most modern scholars believe that each epic is substantially the work of one individual – R.D. Dawe (below) strongly disagrees – but debate whether both are the work of the same individual. Both epics are certainly the product of hundreds of years of traditional, oral story-telling.

They are also very different. The *Iliad* is an intense study of an almost psychopathic Achilles, set in the stifling atmosphere of battle (the Trojan War). The *Odyssey* has more of a romantic-folktale tinge, as, with many an adventure, Odysseus returns from Troy and, disguised as a beggar, plots to win back his wife.

His return takes him ten years (on top of ten years at Troy): three in adventures on the high seas (the Lotus Easters, the Cyclops, Circe, the Underworld, the Sirens, Scylla and Charybdis) and seven trapped with the passionate sea-nymph Calypso. This is folk-tale, Sinbad-the-sailor stuff, adapted to the character and circumstances of a Greek heroic epic tradition. (Take the Cyclops story. There are over 200 versions of this tale from all over the world, all with subtle differences arising from the culture in which the story is located. The one from Thirsk in north Yorkshire, for example, has Jack working in a mill owned by a one-eyed giant and making his escape because he wants to visit Topcliffe Fair.) Meanwhile, at home in Ithaca, 108 suitors are courting Odysseus' wife Penelope while eating him out of house and home. When he finally returns home, folk-tale turns into an epic of revenge, set not on the battlefield but in the household.

But how to control such a diverse, wide-ranging story? An outstanding feature of the structure of the *Odyssey* is the cunning way in which Homer covers this twenty-year span in a narrative time-span of a few weeks, to include everything from Odysseus' marriage to Penelope and birth of their son Telemachus, through the ten-year Trojan War and Odysseus' ten years of travel home, to his final revenge on the suitors. He does this by locating the action in Ithaca at the moment when Odysseus is about to return (although almost everyone has given him up for lost) and by using flashbacks and characters' recollections to cover the previous twenty years. So:

In Book 1, the story opens with Odysseus' only son Telemachus in despair, wondering how much longer he can survive the suitors' depredations, and being sent by Athene to question Nestor and Menelaus (survivors of the Trojan War) about the chances of Odysseus' survival.

In Book 5, the scene now changes to Odysseus, who is about to leave Calypso's cave, where he has been a virtual prisoner for the past seven years, and set off home. We follows his adventures on the high seas as far as Phaeacia, where he finds help and hospitality, and in a famous flashback (**Books 9-12**) describes how he made the journey from Troy to Calypso and thence to Phaeacia (this flashback covers his adventures with the Cyclops, etc.).

In Book 13, Odysseus finally arrives home in Ithaca.

In Book 15, we transfer to Telemachus now returning from his travels.

In Book 16, the two are united; and from now on the story follows a single thread – the punishment of the suitors and Odysseus' reunion with Penelope. It is an elegant, highly sophisticated and (with its flashbacks and accounts of personal memories of the past) much imitated narrative structure.

The *Odyssey* has the sea in its blood:

… They sprang to orders,
hoisting the pinewood mast, they stepped it firm
in its block amidships, lashed it fast with stays
and with braided rawhide halyards hauled the white sail high.
Suddenly wind hit full and the canvas bellied out
and a dark blue wave, foaming up at the bow,
sang out loud and strong as the ship made way,
skimming the whitecaps, cutting towards her goal.
(Robert Fagles, *Homer: The Odyssey*, Viking, 1996)

The *Odyssey* has the household in its blood. Here the faithful old maidservant Eurycleia gives the orders in Odysseus' palace:

'Come now, be quick to sweep and damp the hall;
throw purple fabrics on the shapely chairs;
let others of you sponge the tables, scour
the vessels, and two-handled cups, while some
fetch water from the well.'
(Allen Mandelbaum, *Homer: The Odyssey*, California, 1990)

The *Odyssey* casts loving light on the lowly and humble, especially those who remain loyal to Odysseus in his absence. Here Odysseus' son Telemachus (with whom the *Odyssey* starts) decides to go in search of his long-lost father:

So he spoke and his dear nurse Eurycleia shrieked aloud
and lamenting spoke winged words:
'What is this plan that is in your mind, dear child?
Where do you wish to travel over much territory,
a loved, only son? He was destroyed far from his native land
– divinely-born Odysseus – in a strange region.
And on your going these men [*the suitors*] will at once devise evils
  in the future,
so that you will perish by deceit, and they themselves will divide
  up all these things.
But stay here, settled, in charge of your own possessions. There is
  no need at all for you
to suffer evils or wander over the unwearied sea.'
(P.V. Jones, *Homer: Odyssey 1 and 2*, Aris and Phillips, 1991)

Compared with the *Iliad*, however, the gods are kept in the background. They appear only in disguise (unlike the *Iliad*) while Zeus is now almost a god of justice, arguing that wicked men (e.g. the suitors) deserve the divine punishment they get – most un*Iliad*ic. Here at the start of the *Odyssey* Zeus cites the example of Aegisthus. While Agamemnon was away at the Trojan War, Aegisthus married Agamemnon's wife, though the gods warned him not to, and then killed Agamemnon on his return:

'Well now, how indeed mortal men do blame the gods!
They say it is from us evils come, yet they themselves
By their own recklessness have pains beyond their lot.
So this Aigisthos married beyond his lot the lawful

Wife of the son of Atreus [*Agamemnon*], and killed him on his return;
Knowing he would be destroyed, since we told him beforehand:
We had sent sharp-eyed Hermes, the slayer of Argos,
To tell him not to kill the man and not to woo his wife ...
So Hermes told him; but though of good mind himself, he did not
Change Aigisthos' mind. And now he has paid for it all.'
(Albert Cook, *The Odyssey: Homer*, Norton, New York, 1974)

All this suits a more social, domestic, realistic world of peace, where ethical behaviour is at a premium.

The single outstanding exception to the law of divine distance is Odysseus' patron goddess Athene, who has the closest relationship with her favourite. Here Odysseus has at last arrived home. She approaches him in disguise to help him, and Odysseus tells her a long, false tale. Athene signals that it is she by adopting another disguise and comments, amusingly:

'It would one with eye to profit and a thief who could go beyond you in all tricks, even if a god met him. Hard man, subtle of thought, insatiable in trickery, evidently you were not going, even when you were in your own land, to give up deceptions and trick stories, which are fundamentally dear to you. But come, let us speak about this no longer, since both of us know all about taking profit: you are far the best of all mortals in making plans and using words, and I am well known among all gods for my shrewdness and taking profit.'
(R.D. Dawe, *The Odyssey*, The Book Guild, 1993. This passage is printed in smaller type in Dawe's wonderfully argumentative edition, because he believes the passage has been added to a text originally designed to run without it.)

The *Odyssey* presents us with a different sort of hero too – as one would expect in such a different world from the *Iliad*'s. 'Much enduring' and 'cunning' are two of the commonest epithets for Odysseus in the *Odyssey*. He needs to be.

Consider, for example, how Odysseus handles Polyphemus, the Cyclops ('round-eye'). This one-eyed, man-eating giant has trapped Odysseus and his companions in his cave, and is slowly consuming them. The door to the cave is unbudgeable ('twenty-two fine four-

18

wheeled wagons could not shift it', though Polyphemus puts it in place 'as easily as putting the lid on a quiver'). Further, Polyphemus, though a bit of a loner, has neighbouring Cyclopes who would certainly come to his help in time of trouble.

Brute force versus cunning intelligence – which will win? Odysseus has some vintage wine with him, which he offers Polyphemus. Odysseus is telling the story:

> ... and he took the bowl and he drank and was greatly
> Pleased with drinking the wine, and again he asked me a question:
> 'Give me to drink once more of your goodwill and give me your
>   name now.
> Tell me at once and then I shall give you a gift to delight you ...
> This is a liquor distilled from ambrosia surely and nectar.'
> Thus did he speak; so I brought him the sparkling wine and he
>   drank it;
> Thrice did I bring it and thrice did the Cyclops drink in his folly.
> Now, when the wine began to encompass the wits of the giant,
> Then indeed did I speak these soothing words to the Cyclops:
> 'Since you are asking me what is my famous name, I will tell you,
> Cyclops, and you must give me the gift for a guest that you promised.
> NOMAN is my name, and so my father and mother,
> All my companions also, they all address me as NOMAN.'
> (Brian Kemball-Cook, Homer: The Odyssey, 1993, 12 Francis
> Close, Hitchin SG4 9EJ)

At which point Polyphemus, sozzled and belching up wine and bits of human flesh, collapses in a drunken stupor.

Odysseus now puts his masterplan into action. Heating a sharpened stake in the fire, he and his men drive it into Polyphemus' single eye, spinning it like a drill

> till the blood boiled up round the burning wood. The scorched
> heat singed his lids and brow all round, while his eyeball blazed
> and the very roots crackled in the flame. The Cyclops' eye hissed
> round the olive stake in the same way that an axe or adze hisses
> when a smith plunges it into cold water to quench and strengthen
> the iron. He gave a dreadful shriek, which echoed round the rocky

walls, and we backed away from him in terror, while he pulled the stake from his eye, streaming with blood.

Polyphemus now calls to his neighbours for help and they solicitously enquire what violence is being done to him. But:

> Out of the cave came mighty Polyphemus' voice in reply: 'O my friends, it's Nobody's treachery, not violence, that is doing me to death.' 'Well then,' came the immediate reply, 'if you are alone and nobody is assaulting you, you must be sick and sickness comes from almighty Zeus and cannot be helped. All you can do is to pray to your father, the Lord Poseidon.'
> And off they went, while I laughed to myself at the way my cunning *notion* of a false name had taken them in.
> (E.V. Rieu, revised by D.C.H. Rieu, *Homer: The Odyssey*, Penguin, 1991)

'Notion' is the best one can do with the Homeric pun here. The Greek says literally 'how my name and brilliant *mêtis* deceived them': *mêtis* means 'cunning', and *mê tis* means 'Noman/Nobody'.

This is a wonderful trick. Polyphemus is still able to move the door (he must – the flocks need pasturing). He cannot see Odysseus' next move. His neighbours think he is deranged. So Odysseus and his men escape next morning under the sheep.

One cannot quite imagine Achilles, the obsessive hero of the *Iliad*, behaving like this. In the heroes of the *Iliad* and *Odyssey*, then, Homer has constructed two of the great contrasting voices of literature to echo down the ages: the fiercely uncompromising individual who will be himself whatever the consequences, and the quick-thinking, adaptable, realistic, survivor.

Homer is first and best. This nowadays is called 'privileging' one thing over another and is, evidently, a Bad Thing. But 'privileging' is simply a synonym for 'exercising judgement' or 'discriminating', which I should think was a Good Thing. Greeks would entirely agree. They spent all their lives 'privileging' one thing over another. They too thought Homer first and best, so we are in good company.

It is worth, then, pausing and considering what it is about Homer that so appealed to the Greeks. Essentially, Greeks regarded him as the ultimate teacher of what it meant to be a real Greek. In other words, he

perfectly summarised what Greeks aspired to be. We may identify five major points:

- Homeric man is aristocratic, often with a healthy streak of divine blood somewhere in the veins.
- Homeric man is competitive. Nothing is more important to him than winning, both battles and arguments (over a third of Homer consists of people talking to each other).
- Homeric man is passionate about his honour and status - the way other people look at and rank him.
- Homeric man is aware of the power of the gods, but strives to be as independent of them as possible.
- For all his self-confidence and brilliance, Homeric man knows, or learns, that life is never predictable.

These values and aspirations inform the whole of Greek life, thought and literature.

The translations

Fagles is very rhetorical, Mandelbaum plainer and quieter. Dawe, a Cambridge don, happily admits his translation is 'entirely devoid of literary merit' and the accompanying commentary 'a pretty grim affair' (nonsense: it is terrific fun). They both come in a witty, fascinating and infuriating 879-page volume which takes the *Odyssey* apart (in English) in the best traditions of nineteenth-century analytical scholarship. Kemball-Cook maintains strict Homeric hexameter form throughout. The revised Rieu (introduction by Peter Jones) is more accurate than the 1946 original without losing its spirit. Albert Cook keeps to the Homeric line, translating clearly and close to the original. Peter Jones' *Odyssey 1 and 2* offers Greek text, facing-page, very literal translation, and commentary on the translation.

Newcomers to the *Odyssey* could perhaps miss out Books 2-4 to start with. The authenticity of 23.296 to the end is questionable.

3

Personal Poetry

As we have seen, the first literature of the West was epic poetry, Homer's *Iliad* and *Odyssey*, composed around 700 BC. But these were 'first' only because it was *c*. 700 BC that Greeks began to use writing. Epic poetry had in fact been recited for hundreds of years before writing was ever invented.

So had personal poetry, which had its origins in folksong. While epic poetry focussed on the heroic exploits of the deep past – blood and battles, gods and heroes, tragedy and high drama – personal poetry dealt with the poets' own everyday concerns:

> The moon has set, the Pleiades [*a group of stars*]
> have set; and the night's at halfway,
> and the time is passing,
> and I lie in my bed, alone.
> (Richmond Lattimore, *Greek Lyrics*, Chicago, 1960)

But these are not the private maunderings of whey-faced artistes communing weedily with their souls. Greeks could not care less about artistes' souls. What they did care about was technically brilliant poetry.

Like Homer's epics, personal poetry was for public performance. It was designed to be sung to an instrument (often a lyre – hence 'lyric'), at social gatherings (the *symposium*, the male drinking-party). Love, drink, politics, sport, friends and enemies, life and death feature strongly in it. It still reads today with astonishing vividness. These are real people speaking to us. Whether the incidents described were actually true of the poet's life is, of course, impossible to tell. But that does not matter. It was what the poet wanted his friends to hear. Pleasure was the aim.

Since ancient Greek personal poetry is of extraordinarily high quality, it is all the more infuriating that we have so little of it, mostly

23

fragments. The reason is that no complete manuscripts survived into the Middle Ages (as they did for Homer, for example) when printing was invented. All we have are quotations in authors that do survive (often because they make a pithy point or record an unusual word), plus occasional random fragments that emerge from excavations. It is rather as if, in 5000 AD, no book of W.B. Yeats' poetry existed: all that was known of him was quotations of his works in writers, dictionaries and dictionaries of quotations, and perhaps the odd charred fragment recovered from the site of an ancient book dump.

Archilochus (early seventh century BC) was very highly regarded in the ancient world. He was a military man. Here he tells how he lost his shield:

> Some Saian [*a tribe in Thrace*] sports my splendid shield:
>   I had to leave it in a wood,
> but saved my skin. Well, I don't care –
>   I'll get another just as good.
> (Martin West, *Greek Lyric Poetry*, World's Classics, 1993)

Hardly the sentiment of a Homeric hero – but this pictures a real soldier on a real campaign, perhaps ambushed while asleep and prudently running for it.

Here Archilochus muses on appearances, which were so important to Homer's heroes:

> I do not like the captain, tall-standing, legs apart,
>   Whose cut of hair and whisker is his principal renown.
> Give me the little fellow, with the bigness in his heart,
>   And let his legs be bandy, if they never let him down.
> (D.L. Page)

Many of his listeners doubtless agreed.
Here he ruminates on capacities to survive:

> The fox knows lots of tricks,
> the hedgehog only one – a winner.
> (West)

3. Personal Poetry

Here are some of the milder sexual fragments, in which lyric poetry abounds (boys and women were freely available at *symposia*):

> Up and down she bounced
> like a kingfisher flapping on a jutting rock.

> ... a growth between the thighs ...

> I won't use surgery,
> I know another sovereign remedy
> for a growth of this description.
> (West)

Good, sexy writing and good, sexy jokes have been around for a very long time. The fragmentary nature of the material often makes it all the more suggestive. Here fragments of the crudely laddish Hipponax (sixth century BC) describe a session with the mistress of his enemy Bupalus (... indicates a gap in the papyrus):

> On the floor ... undressing
> we bit and kissed ...
> keeping a look-out through the doors ...
> in catch ... should catch us naked ...
> She was eagerly ...
> while I was fucking ...
> pulling out to the tip, like skinning a sausage,
> saying to hell with Bupalus ...
> Straightway she ... me out and I ...
> Now after our exertions we had ...
> (West)

Cool down with a long drink of barley-water and fill in the gaps yourself.

Of all personal poets, the one we probably value most is Sappho (late seventh century BC, Greek *Psappho*) – a very rare woman's voice among all the men. The Greek epigrammatist Plato called her 'the tenth muse'.

These two exquisite fragments probably come from a wedding hymn, and refer to the bride who kept (or lost?) her virginity before marriage:

25

Just as the sweetest apple reddens high on the branch-top,
High on the topmost branch, forgotten there by the pickers -
Only it wasn't really forgotten, the pickers just couldn't
Reach it ...

Just as the hyacinth up in the mountains is trampled under-
-Foot by shepherds, and the purple flower lies upon the ground ...
(Robert Chandler, *Sappho*, Everyman, 1998)

Here are fragments about love:

... Love shook my heart as a gale
Falls upon trees on a mountainside ...

Love, the loosener of limbs, now shakes me again,
Bitter-sweet and untameable beast ...
(Chandler)

Sappho came from the Greek island of Lesbos, and her reputation has given 'lesbianism' its name. She certainly expresses the most passionate feelings for the girls to whom she is attracted. Here she tries to describe her feelings:

It seems that man is equal to the gods,
that is, whoever sits opposite you
and, drawing nearer, savours, as you speak,
the sweetness of your voice

and the thrill of your laugh, which have so stirred the heart
in my own breast, that whenever I catch
sight of you, even if for a moment,
then my voice deserts me

and my tongue is struck silent, a delicate fire
suddenly races underneath my skin,
my eyes sees nothing, my ears whistle like
the whirling of a top

and sweat pours down me and a trembling creeps over
my whole body, I am greener than grass,
at such times, I seem to be no more than
a step away from death.
(Josephine Balmer, *Sappho*, Bloodaxe Books, 1984)

There is no jealousy of the man here. The man is merely the point of departure for the real subject of the poem – Sappho's blunt description of the powerful, contradictory physical reactions she has when she sees this woman. What an insensitive dolt the 'god-like' man must be to feel nothing! Meanwhile most of her senses are affected – hearing, touch, sight, feeling – but to diminish, rather than heighten, the joy of passion. It almost seems to kill her.

Perhaps the most striking feature of Sappho's attitude to love is her lack of self-pity at its torments, and her desire to help others in the same plight. Here a girl is about to leave the group:

She was leaving me with many tears and said this: 'Oh what bad luck has been ours, Sappho: truly I leave you against my will.' I replied to her thus: 'Go and fare well and remember me, for you know how we cared for you. If not, why then, I want to remind you ... and the good times we had ... You had put on many wreaths of violets and roses (and crocuses?) together by my side, and round your tender neck you put many woven garlands made from flowers and ... with much flowery perfume, fit for a queen, you anointed yourself ... and on soft beds ... you would satisfy your longing ... There was neither ... nor shrine ... from which we were absent, no grove ... nor dance ... sound'
(D.A. Campbell, *Greek Lyric 1*, Loeb no. 142, Harvard-Heinemann, 1982)

Note how Sappho enumerates their past joys to help the girl (and Sappho?) come to term with their present unhappiness.

By contrast Ibycus, a sixth-century BC Greek from Reggio in Italy, found love impossible to handle. In one famous fragment, it descends on him like a storm wind from the north. Here he imagines love trapping him like an animal in Aphrodite's (the Cyprian's) hunting-net; and he trembles at its approach like an old, exhausted race-horse:

Again Love, looking at me meltingly from under his dark eyelids, hurls me with his manifold enchantments into the boundless nets of the Cyprian. How I fear his onset, as a prize-winning horse still bearing the yoke in his old age goes unwillingly with swift chariot to the race.
(Campbell, vol. 3)

Anacreon (early sixth century BC) was renowned for drinking and womanising to a fine old age. His poems frequently have a sting in the tail. Note the 'anacreontic' rhythm of this translation – ti ti tum ti tum ti tum tum:

> I have gone grey at the temples.
> yes, my head, it's white, there's nothing,
> of the grace of youth that's left me,
> and my teeth are like an old man's.
> Life is lovely. But the lifetime
> that remains for me is little.
> For this cause I mourn. The terrors
> of the Dark Pit never leave me.
> For the house of Death is deep down
> underneath; the downward journey
> to be feared, for once I go there
> I know well there's no returning.
> (Lattimore)

Where, you ask, is the sting in the tail? Unfortunately, Lattimore misses the joke: in the last line there is a sexual *double entendre*, best got in English by 'I know well I won't get up again'. One can easily imagine an ageing Anacreon putting on a mournful face to sing this poem, his fellow partygoers at the *symposium* beginning to feel sorry for the poor old boy, and then laughing their heads off at the last line.

Boys and girls were both fair game to Anacreon. Here he invents a famous image, the charioteer of the soul:

> O lad with the look of a lass,
> I seek you, but you don't heed,
> not knowing you hold the reins
> of my soul, my life.
> (West)

3. Personal Poetry

Here he works up a superb image of a filly needing an experienced rider (enjoy the rhythm):

Thracian filly, why so sharply
shy away with sidelong glances,
    thinking I've no expertise?
Be assured, I'd put your bit on
smartly, hold the reins and run you
    round the limits of the course.
But for now you graze the meadows,
frisk and play, for want of any
    good experienced riding man.
(West)

We have concentrated on love and sex because these are so much associated in our minds with personal poetry. But the genre in fact covers a huge range of topics. Xenophanes (late sixth century BC) complains at the credit given to brawn over brains ('just because there's some champion boxer in town, or wrestler, or pentathlon man, or runner, that won't improve law and order') and mocks at anthropomorphic gods ('if oxen, horses and lions could draw, horses would draw gods like horses …'). Simonides (early fifth century BC) argues that men's luck never lasts ('not even the wing-spreading house-fly/changes perch so fast'). Alcaeus, a contemporary of Sappho and deeply involved in the politics of Lesbos, found himself exiled as he made a stand against one popular leader after another, and sang his political misfortune to his male friends at *symposia* ('Now we must drink with might and main,/ get drunk, for Myrsilus is dead!'; but then 'Fitznobody Pittacus/they've made tyrant of that ill-starred and gutless town/ with united acclaim').

This genre, established over 2,500 years ago, is as lively today as ever it was (think of Wendy Cope and Gavin Ewart, for example). But it is worth noting that, like Homer, it is the product of Greeks living on the coast of western Turkey and the Greek islands. The Greek cultural revolution, in this case turning folk-song into high literary art, took place outside Athens and the Greek mainland. Athens' turn comes later.

Classics in Translation

The translations

M.L. West is a fellow of All Souls, Oxford. His *Greek Lyric Poetry* is easily the best introduction to the subject, containing poems and fragments of nearly 40 personal poets, with notes. Balmer's fine *Sappho* contains most of what remains of Sappho and can be made sense of (again, with notes). Chandler's *Sappho* also contains earlier translations and adaptations of the poetess. Lattimore's *Greek Lyrics* is rather a mixed bag. The excellent new Loeb editions of *Greek Lyric* (by D.A. Campbell) provide full Greek texts and facing-page translations of Sappho (in vol. 1) with the ancient evidence for her life. D.A. Campbell's *The Golden Lyre* (Duckworth) is a good general survey (all Greek translated).

4

Aeschylus

Ancient Greek poetry like Homer's and Sappho's which we have looked at in the last three chapters was not composed to be read by lonely highbrows ruminating pensively in shady nook or study. It was individually composed to be chanted or sung, solo, before a passionately enthusiastic audience, at public performance or private drinking party, to lyre or oboe (Greek *aulos*) accompaniment. Acclaim through live performance was the name of the artistic game in the ancient world.

Greek tragedy was an equally live performance, but of a rather different sort. Take the following. Oedipus, king of Thebes, is dead. In his last breath he had cursed his two sons to die at each other's hand in battle. His sons are now at war with each other over the succession. Eteocles is defending Thebes, his impious brother Polyneices attacking it. Thebes has seven gates, and each side has seven champions. A messenger describes the champion that Polyneices has assigned to attack each gate, and gate by gate Eteocles details one of his own warriors in defence. The messenger now announces that the seventh gate will be attacked by Polyneices – the very gate that Eteocles is defending!

> *Eteocles*: O house that gods drive mad, that gods so deeply hate,
> O house of endless tears, our house of Oedipus!
> It is his curse that now bears fruit in us his sons …
> I will go forth and face him – I myself.
> Who has a stronger right than I? Chief against chief
> I'll match him, brother to brother, enemy to enemy.
> *Chorus*: Never, beloved master, son of Oedipus!
> Why must your mood match your brother's blasphemies?
> It is enough that Cadmeans [*men of Thebes*] fight hand to hand
> With men of Argos; blood so shed can be appeased.
> But your two bloods are one: such brother-murdering
> Not through an age of time could such pollution fade.

31

Eteocles: If fate must be endured, let it come free from shame.
What else is there to glory in, among the dead?
But doom joined with dishonour strikes your last hope dumb.
Chorus (*sings and dances*): My son, what are you bent upon?
Do not let bursting passion
And lust for battle carry you away.
This urge that you feel is evil –
Banish it before it grows.
Eteocles: This act moves swiftly to a head; Heaven wills it so;
Then let the wind of doom, Hell's tide and Apollo's hate [*god of prophecy*]
Bear down to ruin Oedipus' race to the last man.
(P. Vellacott, *Aeschylus: Prometheus and other plays*, Penguin, 1961, slightly altered)

This is from the climax of Aeschylus' *Seven Against Thebes* (467 BC). It is an overwhelmingly powerful play: when the Chorus asks if Eteocles is prepared to spill a brother's blood, he replies 'the gods care nothing for us' and departs to arm himself for death. Eteocles' fatal determination reminds us of Achilles in the *Iliad*, and Aeschylus was indeed said to 'feast on scraps from Homer's table'.

But where does tragedy come from? Who invented it? What is this 'Chorus'? Why does it suddenly break out into song and dance?

Homer and personal poetry, as we have seen, are matters of solo performance. At great public celebrations like religious festivals, however, massed choirs, not solo song, were the order of the day. Here songs about gods and heroes of the past were composed for choral presentation, accompanied by instruments and dancing (a choir which sang and danced was called a chorus). Pindar (*c.* 520-440 BC) wrote such songs on commission, to celebrate winners at the great athletic festivals like the Olympic Games. He would liken the winner to some fabulous mythic hero, often to warn him against getting too big for his trainers.

Unfortunately, little of the music itself actually survives – only fourteen tiny fragments from the Greek period. From what we can gather, it seems to have consisted in rather jazzy weaving about in a narrow melodic compass, without harmonisation (and so choral singing was in unison). Music for snake-charmers in B movies comes to mind. But what has all this got to do with Aeschylus (525-455 BC)? A very great deal.

4. Aeschylus

Aeschylus is one of the very earliest Greek tragedians, and tragedy seems to have developed out of choruses singing and dancing in honour of Dionysus, god of transformation – and so god of wine and intoxication, ecstasy, impersonation, masks and therefore the theatre. At some stage, it seems, someone (Thespis, Greeks thought) decided to add a prologue and a speaking part to the chorus. As a result, what was originally just a song and dance about mythic gods and heroes now became an enactment of a story, played out between chorus and speaking actor (presumably masked to look the part). What with all the song, dance, action, masks and colourful costumes, Greek tragedy bore no relation to (let us say) a production in white sheets of Christ's passion at a convent. It was also competitive – tragedians competed against each other to win festival prizes.

In other words, Greek tragedy looked and sounded like a sort of masked musical. Aeschylus added a second actor, Sophocles a third, and there you have the basic personnel of the Greek tragedy: a chorus of twelve or fifteen, mostly singing and dancing its part in unison, and three actors, mostly speaking theirs (they sometimes break out into solo song). The typical shape of a tragedy became a scene-setting prologue and then a series of alternating choral songs and spoken scenes.

What 'tragedy' has got to do with all this is a very good question. The word means literally 'goat-song' (*tragos*, goat; *ôidê*, song, ode), or 'song somehow connected with goats'. But goats rarely take top billing on the tragic stage. Perhaps goat sacrifices originally accompanied songs to Dionysus? We can only guess.

Tragedy was invented perhaps *c.* 530 BC and Aeschylus' first production was in 499 BC. Our first surviving play of his is *Persians* (472 BC), our last the famous *Oresteia* trilogy (458 BC). There is no doubt that Aeschylus was a genius. Tragedy had been in existence for only perhaps seventy years when he produced *Oresteia*, a theatrical masterpiece of the very highest order.

To the modern ear and eye, it is true, it may seem inflexible and archaic – great long choruses, great long speeches, stilted dialogue, much of it between actor and chorus rather than actor and actor, and all that groaning and lamenting. Tom Stoppard it certainly ain't. Even worse, perhaps, is the mythic background – meat and drink to Greeks, but to us putting up an impenetrable barrier of incomprehensible (and unpronounceable) names, places, events and situations. All of which is fair comment if you read it. But tragedy was not meant to be read. It was meant to be performed, and in performance the problems fade away: a turkey on the page becomes an eagle on the stage.

Aeschylus' *Agamemnon*, the first play of the *Oresteia* trilogy, begins when King Agamemnon is on the point of returning home to Argos after winning the Trojan War. But as the watchman who opens the play indicates, all is not well, even though he has just seen the beacon that indicates Troy has fallen:

> Now this beacon watching has thrown triple six for me!
> Well, may it come to pass that the lord of the house
> comes back, and that I clasp his well-loved hand in mine.
> But for the rest I am silent; a great ox stands
> upon my tongue; but the house itself, if it could find a voice,
> could tell the tale most truly; for I of my choice
> speak to those who know; but for those who do not know, I forget.
> (H. Lloyd-Jones, *Aeschylus: Oresteia*, Duckworth, 1982)

Observe how the watchman refers to the house as if it could speak (and, figuratively, it will when Agamemnon's death cries ring out of it). This may have been the first time that the backdrop was a palace. Aeschylus' dramatic imagination is already making it work to the full.

Enter the Chorus, old men of Argos, and they too are full of foreboding. They remember that Agamemnon had had to sacrifice his daughter Iphigeneia in order to get the wind for Troy:

> 'My father, father!' – she might pray to the winds;
> no innocence moves her judges mad for war.
> Her father called his henchmen on,
>   on with a prayer,
>   'Hoist her over the altar
> like a yearling, give it all your strength!
> She's fainting – lift her,
>   sweep her robes around her,
> but slip this strap in her gentle, curving lips ...
>   here, gag her hard, a sound will curse the house.'
> (Robert Fagles, *Aeschylus: The Oresteia*, Penguin, 1977)

And now we meet Iphigeneia's mother, queen Clytaemnestra ('a woman who thinks like a man', as the watchman said of her) and our fears

4. Aeschylus

35

increase, as she starts to talk in most ambiguous language about her desire for her husband Agamemnon's return:

> God grant we see them safe!
> If the fleet sails free from the taint of sin, the gods
> may grant them safely to retrace their outward course –
> those whom no wakeful anger of the forgotten dead
> waits to surprise with vengeance ...
>   These are a woman's words.
> May good prevail beyond dispute, in sight of all!
> My life holds many blessings; I would enjoy them now.
> (P. Vellacott, *Aeschylus: The Oresteian Trilogy*, Penguin, 1959)

Gulp, we think. The Chorus now sing of Trojan Paris's folly in seducing Spartan Helen, an event that started the Trojan War and ended in Troy's destruction. In an unmatched sequence of odes, they reflect on Ares, god of war, who weighs out men's bodies as men weigh out gold:

> Geldshark Ares god of War
> broker of men's bodies
> usurer of living flesh
> corpse-trafficker that god is –
>
> give to WAR your men's fleshgold
> and what are your returns?
> kilos of cold clinker packed
> in army-issue urns
>
> wives mothers sisters each one scans
> the dogtags of the amphorae [*Greek urns*]
> which grey ashes are my man's?
> they sift the jumbled names and cry:
>
> *my husband sacrificed his life*
> my brother's a battle-martyr
> aye, for someone else's wife –
> Helen, whore of Sparta!'
> (Tony Harrison, *Oresteia*, Rex Collings, 1982)

But then, what happened to Iphigeneia …?

A messenger arrives to announce the army's imminent return, despite a stormy and difficult journey home. Clytaemnestra can hardly wait. The chorus sing further of Helen, but what (we think) of Agamemnon? What justice awaits him?

> Hands bespattered with shed blood
> raise gilded rafters to the skies
> Justice searching for the good
> leaves with averted eyes
>
> Justice doesn't kneel to fame
> kiss affluence's feet
> isn't dazzled by a name
> gold-coined but counterfeit
>
> Justice isn't put out of her stride
> Justice can't be turned aside

ENTER AGAMEMNON
(Harrison)

If this is not a master-dramatist at work, I'm Clint Eastwood.

And it gets better. Agamemnon is effusively welcomed into the house by the scheming Clytaemnestra, and is easily persuaded to tread on purple as he goes (an honour reserved only for gods) to demonstrate publicly his weakness, gullibility and vanity. We keenly await his death screams, followed by a speech from a distraught messenger describing what has happened.

We get nothing of the sort. Instead, there comes into focus Agamemnon's Trojan mistress Cassandra. She was a prophetess who had rejected Apollo's advances and been doomed by him always to tell the truth and never to be believed. Cassandra had entered with Agamemnon in his chariot, but remained silent throughout. Now Clytaemnestra orders her in too, to share Agamemnon's fate. It is at this point that Cassandra bursts into song, foreseeing in ghastly detail everything that will happen in the palace when she goes in and linking it to the house's past – and, inevitably, not being believed. It is a scene of simply stunning power, unmatched in Greek tragedy – and does away with the need for a messenger speech after the event (though naturally we get one, in the mouth of Clytaemnestra, who, covered in blood, 'black showers of murderous dew', comes in to exult in what she has done).

In any terms this is amazing theatre (and Clytaemnestra, in particular, an astonishing conception in a world where, scholars sagely assure us, women were feeble, powerless, downtrodden creatures). Here are some extracts from the end of Cassandra scene as she approaches the palace and her death; and Clytaemnestra's subsequent speech, with her typically extraordinary language:

Cassandra: Why do I lament so piteously?
Since I have seen my native city, Ilion,
suffer the way it did, and those who captured Troy
ending like this under the verdict of the gods,
I'll go; I will begin the rite; I can endure my death.
Now I address these doors as those that lead to Hades;
May I meet one lethal stroke
so I may close my eyes without a struggle,
as my blood streams from me in easy death.
Chorus Elder: You are a lady greatly to be pitied; wise as well,
in your long speech. But if you truly know
that you yourself will die, how can you tread the path
towards the altar with the courage of an ox driven by gods?
[*An ox was the normal sacrificial animal. Cassandra foresees a different 'sacrifice'.*]
Cassandra: Strangers, there's no escape for any further time.
Elder: Last moments are the highest valued.
Cassandra: This day has come. I gain nothing by flight.
Elder: Your constancy's the mark of a courageous soul.
Cassandra: Fortunate people never have to hear such words.
Elder: Still, a glorious death brings fame.
Cassandra: Oh, my father, and your noble children!
[*i.e. Priam, king of Troy, his many children all now dead.*]
Elder: What is it? What fear turns you back?
Cassandra: Oh! Oh!
Elder: Why d'you cry out? Some horror in your mind?
Cassandra: This house breathes out a bloody stench of murder.
Elder: That's the smell of sacrifices at the hearth.
Cassandra: The reek is putrid like that from a grave.

4. Aeschylus

(Cassandra exits; death screams are heard; the Chorus is paralysed; enter Clytaemnestra, with both bodies, Agamemnon's enmeshed in a net-like robe.)

> *Clytaemnestra*: Much have I said before to suit the moment, and
> I'm not ashamed to contradict it all;
> how else could anyone contrive hostilities against an enemy
> who seemed to be a friend [*i.e. Agamemnon*], and fence the
>   hunting-nets
> of pain up to a height beyond escape?
> This conflict is the climax of an ancient feud –
> it's long been in my mind, but still at last it came.
> I stand just where I struck; the deed's been done.
> And I will not deny that I made sure
> he had no chance to escape or ward off his fate.
> I cast an endless mesh around him, like
> a net for fish – a rich and evil robe.
> I strike him twice, and with two cries
> his limbs went slack, and when he'd fallen
> I gave him a third, a votive offering
> of thanks to Pluto, saviour of the dead.
> And as he lies he breathes his life away,
> and blowing out a rapid spurt of blood
> he strikes me with black showers of murderous dew,
> [*the image here is almost orgasmic*]
> and I rejoice no less than does the growing corn
> in Zeus' rain during the birth-pangs of the sheaf.
> Elders of Argos, this is how things are;
> be glad if that's your will, and I will glory openly.
> If it were right to pour [*celebratory*] libations now
> upon this corpse, it would be just, it would be more than just;
> such was the bowl of cursed evils this man filled
> inside our house, and drains it now on his return.
> (Michael Ewans (1995), *Aischylos: The Oresteia*, Everyman)

You will have to read for yourself what happens next and in the rest of this superb trilogy (cf. p. 63). But there will be more to say about tragedy when we look at Sophocles in the next chapter.

The translations

Sir Hugh Lloyd-Jones was Professor of Greek at Oxford. His fairly literal translation is accompanied with excellent introduction and notes. Fagles' translation pays especially close attention to Aeschylus' imagery. Vellacott is readable but does not catch the flavour of Aeschylus' amazing Greek. Tony Harrison, a classicist by training, is a world-famous poet in his own right. His National Theatre translation remains without peer. Michael Ewans' new translation has extremely helpful notes on the stage action.

5

Sophocles

In the last chapter we explored the work of Aeschylus (*c.* 525-455 BC), the first tragic dramatist whose plays survive. Given that tragedy was hardly out of nappies, Aeschylus' understanding of the theatre was remarkable. But it can still read, to us, rather stiffly. With Sophocles (*c.* 495-406 BC), we see something much more like theatre as we understand it. For a start, Sophocles was master of the vivid, three-way conversation (but then he did introduce the third actor).

Here in Sophocles' *Antigone*, Antigone has buried the body of her brother Polyneices against the orders of the king – their uncle, Creon. Antigone's sister Ismene had refused to help her originally, but now Antigone is captured, Ismene wants to play the martyr too:

Chorus: Here comes Ismene, weeping
in sisterly sorrow; a darkened brow,
flushed face, and the fair cheek marred
with flooding rain.
Creon: You crawling viper! Lurking in my house
to suck my blood! Two traitors unbeknown
plotting against my throne. Do you admit
to a share in this burying, or deny all knowledge?
Ismene: I did it – yes – if she will let me say so.
I am as much to blame as she is.
Antigone: No.
That is not just. You would not lend a hand
and I refused your help in what I did.
Ismene: But I am not ashamed to stand beside you
now in your hour of trial, Antigone.
Antigone: Whose was the deed, Death and the dead are witness.
I love no friend whose love is only words.
Ismene: O sister, sister, let me share your death,

41

share in the tribute of honour to him that is dead.
Antigone: You shall not die with me. You shall not claim
that which you would not touch. One death is enough.
(E.F. Watling, *The Theban Plays*, Penguin, 1953)

The 'three actor' rule obviously restricts things. The dramatist can have as many characters as he wants, but with only three actors to play them, he has to make certain (for example) that they have enough time off-stage to change costume for a new part.

Likewise, being the third actor of the (all-male) cast must have felt a bit like being a chameleon on a tartan rug. In *Antigone*, for example, Creon is on stage most of the time, and Antigone for three-quarters of it. So the poor third actor probably had to play Ismene, a guard, Antigone's fiancé, a prophet, and Creon's wife.

At this point it is worth considering the further *narrative* problems that Sophocles – and all ancient tragedians – faced in the light of the conventions governing stage performance. First, stage time was real time: a play lasting one and half hours represented one and half hours in the life of its characters (so how do you deal with the 'past'?). Second, violent or fantastical events could not be staged (they had to 'happen' offstage) – so what will be offstage, what onstage? Third, the backdrop was a static building, usually a palace, tent, hut or cave. How do you stage a tragedy in what is essentially a front-garden? Finally, the Chorus. It will be on-stage almost all the time. Of whom will it consist?

Now imagine you are going to stage the tragedy of (say) Orpheus and Eurydice. Orpheus is a musician who can charm wild animals. He falls in love with Eurydice. She, chased by a molester, is bitten by a snake and dies. He goes down to the underworld to rescue her, charming the nasties as he does so, but is told not to look back at her. As he emerges into the light with her, he cannot resist looking back, and Eurydice disappears down to Hades for ever. Distraught, Orpheus wanders the world, and is finally torn to pieces by bacchant women.

So – what is the tragedy? And therefore which hour and a half? Location? What will be shown onstage, what offstage? What can be reported as 'past', and how? Who will the Chorus be? Will a god come on at the end explaining 'what happened next?' And so on. These are seriously difficult questions. A tragedy, however effortless it looks, does not write itself. There are problems all down the line.

The Greek philosopher Aristotle defined tragedy as dealing with a serious subject. A great man, not too good or too bad, passes from happiness to misfortune, because of some mistake of judgement (*hamartia*). In the process, he moves from delusion to enlightenment (*anagnorisis*); which brings about his reversal in fortune (*peripeteia*).

This judgement is a result of Aristotle's normal inductive method of biological analysis – look at all examples of a species and then try to define it. He had obviously been deeply influenced by Sophocles, because this definition fits Sophocles better than anyone else. For example, one of Sophocles' favourite devices to emphasise his hero's delusion is to fool him with ambiguous dreams, oracles and signs: *we* understand what they mean, but the characters don't – yet. Here in *Oedipus the King* (cited by Aristotle as his 'perfect' tragedy), Oedipus has found himself accused by a prophet of killing the previous king Laius. Oedipus' wife queen Jocasta says he should pay no attention to prophets:

> ... Listen to me,
> and you will learn that the prophetic art
> touches our human fortunes not at all.
> I soon can give you proof. An oracle
> once came to Laius – from the god himself [*Apollo*]
> I do not say, but from his ministers:
> His fate it was that, should he have a son
> by me, that son would take his father's life.
> But Laius was killed – or so they said – by strangers,
> by brigands, at a place where three ways meet.
> As for the child, it was not three days old
> when Laius fastened both its feet together
> and had it cast over a precipice.
> Therefore Apollo failed: for neither did
> his son kill Laius, nor did Laius meet
> the awful end he feared, killed by his son.
> (H.D.F. Kitto, *Sophocles*, World's Classics, 1994)

Jocasta, of course, is utterly deceived: that son survived to become Oedipus, her husband, and it was he, not brigands, who killed Laius. When the appalling truth is revealed, Jocasta commits suicide and Oedipus blinds himself.

Note here how the gods in tragedy differ from epic. Homer's

characters may remain ignorant of divine plans, but *we* know precisely what is going on among the gods because Homer, the narrator, tells us. But there is no narrator in tragedy. As a result, the gods of tragedy seem to us far more mysterious and incomprehensible. Both audience and characters can only grope for understanding.

A further point is worth noting. Many commentators exclaim on Jocasta's impiety here – refusing to believe oracles! A disgrace! Nothing could be further from the truth. Jocasta does not refuse to believe them. All Greeks knew that oracles were very difficult to interpret, that they may appear to say one thing and in fact say something else (cf. Socrates' reaction to a baffling oracle on p. 77). Jocasta's conclusion is that the prophetic art does not touch us – i.e. cannot be dealt with reliably by humans. How can it, since (as it seems to *her*) this oracle has proved wrong? Observe also how she thinks the oracle may not have come from Apollo at all, but 'from his ministers'. This is a pious woman, keen to save Apollo's reputation. The irony of the situation is all the richer for it.

So the gods move in mysterious ways to Sophoclean man (and woman) – but move they do. Here in *Antigone*, king Creon has now condemned Antigone to death for burying her brother's body. As she is led out to die, the Chorus speculate on the havoc the gods wreak on families down the generations. Remember that Antigone was a daughter of Oedipus and his wife/mother Jocasta:

Blest, they are truly blest who all their lives
have never tasted devastation. For others, once
the gods have rocked a house to its foundations
            the ruin will never cease, cresting on and on
from one generation on throughout the race –
like a great mounting tide
driven on by savage northern gales,
            over the dead black depths
boiling up from the bottom dark heaves of sand
and the headlands, taking the storm's onslaught full-force,
roar, and the low moaning
                        echoes on and on
                                    and now
as in ancient times I see the sorrows of the house,
the living heirs of the old ancestral kings,

piling on the sorrows of the dead
       and one generation cannot free the next –
some god will bring them crashing down,
the race finds no release.
(Robert Fagles, *The Three Theban Plays*, Penguin, 1982)

This is powerfully expressed, but these are ancient truths, platitudes almost – hardly original. But then – can we do any better? Who knows how the gods work? This is how Greeks made sense of their own experience.

But if the gods are ruthless, men at least can show pity. In Sophocles' *Ajax*, the armour of the dead Achilles has been awarded not to the great Ajax but to Odysseus. Ajax feels utterly humiliated. That night he goes berserk, driven mad by the goddess Athene and slaughtering sheep and cattle as if they were Greek leaders. In the morning he comes to his senses. Here Athene gloats over the way she has humiliated him:

Athene: Do you see, Odysseus, how great the gods' power is?
Who was more full of foresight than this man,
or abler, do you think, to act with judgement?
Odysseus: None that I know of. Yet I pity
his wretchedness, though he is my enemy,
for the terrible yoke of blindness that is upon him.
I think of him, yet also of myself;
For I see the true state of all us that live –
We are dim shapes, no more, and weightless shadow.
(John Moore, *Sophocles II* (ed. Grene and Lattimore), Chicago, 1957)

From our perspective we may feel Odysseus' pity is a rebuke to the divinity. But ancient gods loved only their favourites.

Sophoclean heroes like Ajax and Oedipus strike us with tremendous power – great oaks of men, whose downfall would not move us so much if their roots were not so deep. In burying her brother against the king's decree, Antigone too moves us for the stand she takes on behalf of the young against the old, the female against the male, the duties of the family against those of the state, the laws of gods against the laws of men. Here Antigone famously explains why she transgressed Creon's orders:

... it was not Zeus who made this proclamation, nor was it Justice who lives with the gods below that established such laws among men, nor did I think your proclamations strong enough to have power to overrule, mortal as they were, the unwritten and unfailing ordinances of the gods. For these have life, not simply today and yesterday, but for ever, and no one knows how long ago they were revealed.

(H. Lloyd-Jones, *Sophocles II*, Loeb Classical Library no. 21, Harvard, 1994)

Tragedy does not deal in answers. It deals in all too human situations, articulated via great heroes of the past, where powerful human wills and sometimes mysterious divine forces clash. It is noticeable that in Greek tragedy it is nearly always within the family that such tragic crises occur. This institution, most precious to ancient Greeks, was also felt to be the most vulnerable and unstable. Greeks sensed that it was to the family that men and women committed their deepest feelings, and that truly tragic violence erupted when the raw nerves of those feelings were exposed, especially by treachery or betrayal.

The family is at the heart of Greek tragedy. That said, there is a strong civic element to it as well. It is no coincidence that it was invented about the same time that democracy was invented by Cleisthenes (in 508 BC). This we shall explore when we consider Euripides.

The translations

Watling is clear, plain and eminently readable. Kitto is closer to the Greek, while Fagles goes for dramatic effect. Moore is part of the useful nine-volume Chicago tragedy series. Lloyd-Jones, in the new Loeb series (with facing-page Greek), is the most literal.

6

Herodotus

The great ancient Greek historian Herodotus (*c.* 490-420 BC) is discussing one of the major events of Greek history, the Trojan War. He cannot believe that the Trojans allowed their city to be besieged for ten years simply because Trojan Paris had seduced the Greek floozie Helen and taken her back to Troy. No, he prefers the Egyptian version of events.

The Egyptian tale, he says, is that Helen was indeed seduced by Paris but, *en route* from Greece to Troy, was blown off-course and landed in Egypt. So when the Greeks arrived at Troy asking for the return of Helen and the Trojans reasonably said 'Sorry about that, squire, can't help you there', the Greeks equally reasonably replied 'Pull the other', and the war began. Herodotus now comments:

> I am inclined to accept [*the Egyptian version*] for the following reason: had Helen really been in Troy, she would have been handed over to the Greeks with or without Paris's consent; for I cannot believe that either Priam [*father of Paris and king of Troy*] or any other kinsman of his was mad enough to be willing to risk his own and his children's lives and the safety of the city, simply to let Paris continue to live with Helen ... the fact is, they did not give Helen up because they had not got her ... This, then, is my interpretation.
> (A. de Selincourt (revised), *Herodotus: The Histories*, Penguin, 1996)

This brief episode shows why Herodotus is known as 'the father of history'. The word 'history' comes from the Greek *historia*, meaning 'enquiry, investigation'. But everything written prior to Herodotus that we might feel tempted to call history is always presented as incontrovertible truth. The Old Testament and Egyptian or Babylonian royal records, for example, never ask questions or admit of doubts. They

47

never say 'I do not know' or 'there are three versions of this event and I'm blowed if I can tell you which is the right one'.

But for Herodotus the past is there to be argued over and debated. He is constantly saying 'That is one account of this event, but there is another which goes as follows ...' and 'I was told this but do not believe it for the following reasons ...'. In other words, he is the first chronicler of the past to start asking serious questions about it and to expect it to come up with reasoned answers. This is one sense in which he is 'father of history'.

There is another important sense too. Herodotus's nine-book *History* leads up to the Persian Wars, the four great battles – Marathon, Thermopylae, Salamis and Plataea, fought between 490-479 BC – in which the Greeks drove back the invading Persian armies. But note how Herodotus begins his *History*:

> Herodotus of Halicarnassus [*modern Bodrum, Turkey*] here displays his enquiry, so that human achievements may not become forgotten in time, and great and marvellous deeds – some displayed by Greeks, some by barbarians [*i.e. non-Greeks*] – may not be without their glory; and especially to show why the two people fought with each other.
> (de Selincourt)

This, in other words, is history with a broad lens. The Persian Wars may have been the Greeks' finest hour, but Herodotus's interest is in Greek and non-Greek alike, and not just in war and politics either. He writes what one might call 'total' history. He is captivated by all 'human achievements'.

Here, for example, Herodotus describes the brilliant Babylonian National Health Service:

> They have no physicians, but when a man is ill, they lay him in a public square, and the passers-by come up to him, and if they have ever had his disease themselves or have known any one who has suffered from it, they give him advice, recommending him to do whatever they found good in their own case, or in the case known to them; and no one is allowed to pass the sick man in silence without asking him what his ailment is.
> (G. Rawlinson, *Herodotus: Histories*, Wordsworth Classics, 1996)

Please, no one tell our Health minister. But wherever Greeks or Persians went prior to their great conflict, Herodotus followed, note-book in hand, eager to know everything about the cultures he encountered. Book Two, for example, is entirely devoted to Egypt. This is how Egyptians catch a crocodile:

> They bait a hook with a chine of pork and let it float out into midstream, and at the same time, standing on the bank, they take a live pig and beat it. The crocodile, hearing its squeals, makes a rush towards it, encounters the bait, gulps it down and is hauled out of the water. The first thing the huntsman does when he has got the beast on land is to plaster its eyes with mud: this done, it is dispatched easily enough.
> (de Selincourt)

Nor, amazingly for an ancient Greek, does Herodotus stint his praise for other cultures. In Egypt, he says, there are 'more monuments which beggar description ... than anywhere else in the world', and praises them for keeping records of the past, which have made them 'much the most learned of any nation of which I have had experience'.

Some cynics in the ancient world, however, far from calling Herodotus 'father of history', preferred to call him 'father of lies', and there is indeed no lack of apparently incredible stories. In Arabia, for example:

> They have two marvellous kinds of sheep, nowhere else found. One of these has tails no less than three cubits [4' 6"] long. Were the sheep to trail these after them, they would suffer hurt by the rubbing of the tails on the ground; but as it is every shepherd there knows enough of carpentry to make little carts which they fix under the tails, binding the tail of each sheep on its own cart ...
> (A.D. Godley, *Herodotus II*, Loeb no. 118, Heinemann-Harvard, 1938)

True or false? True, actually, as John Goodridge explains in *ad familiares* vol. XIII (the journal of *Friends of Classics*). This is not to deny that there is still some pretty odd stuff here and there in Herodotus, but it all adds to the fun – and our sense of Herodotus' utter amazement at the wonder of the world about him, and undiluted pleasure at being able to tell others about it.

6. Herodotus

Since we are used to vast tomes with a huge time-scale, covering world-wide events, it is very easy to take Herodotus' massive work for granted. But, to our knowledge, nothing like a one-man 'scientific' history on this scale existed before Herodotus dreamed it up. With what by our standards would be the crudest of resources and reference works, and to a great extent on the back of his own (as it appears) extensive travels, he constructed a history that began two hundred years before his own time and made sense of a net-work of inter-related events across the whole of the known world, from Spain to India, from South Russia and Georgia to Ethiopia. Intellectually, it is a quite stunning achievement.

The main organising principle behind this great masterpiece is 'a dense web of causal connections created in large part by personal reciprocities that span generations and cultures' (Dewald's introduction in Waterfield, below). Herodotus' thinking goes: 'Why did A do this? Because B had previously done that to him. But why did B do that to him? Because C had done that to B, so that A ...' and so on. As one reads through what often seems (but is not) a chaotic narrative, it become clear that it is the personal connections between peoples and individuals that shape events.

For example, Herodotus' history begins with the Persian account of how east and west first came into conflict. It all started with Phoenicians stealing Greek Io and landing her in Egypt. Greeks then reciprocated by stealing Phoenician Europa, and on top of that abducting Georgian Medea. So Trojan Paris repaid the deed by seducing Greek Helen. Then Greece attacked Troy, and that was what sealed eternal enmity between east and west. Herodotus is not convinced and continues:

> I am not going to come down in favour of this or that account of events, but I will talk about the man who, to my certain knowledge, first undertook acts of criminal aggression against the Greeks. I will show who it was who did this, and then proceed with the rest of the account.
> (R. Waterfield, *Herodotus: The Histories*, World's Classics, 1998)

And off he goes, fingering Croesus, king of Lydia (*c.* 550 BC), as the guilty party, and at once describing how his family came to rule Lydia. It was all down to Candaules, who ... (and here follows the famous story of Candaules who thought his wife the most beautiful woman in

51

the world and invited his personal guard Gyges to see her naked – all of which ended in Gyges, the first of the line that would issue in Croesus, assassinating Candaules and assuming the throne).

Herodotus is very important in another sense too. One of the most original and important marks of early Greek thinkers is their attempt to explain the world without resorting to the supernatural; put another way, to explain human activity purely in human terms. Herodotus comes very close to this ideal. Here, for example, he describes a ravine in Thessaly:

> According to native Thessalian tradition, the ravine through which the Peneius flows was made by Poseidon. This is not implausible, because the sight of this ravine would make anyone who thinks that Poseidon is responsible for earthquakes, and therefore that rifts formed by earthquakes are formed by him, say that it was the work of Poseidon. For it seems to me that this rift in the mountains was caused by an earthquake.
> (Waterfield)

But Herodotus' understanding of history still persuades him that a disruptive divinity controls the affairs of the excessively powerful, enviously determined to bring them low. As a result there is in Herodotus an almost tragic sense of inevitability about the lives of ruthless autocrats. Here, on the eve of his planned invasion of Greece, the arrogant Persian king Xerxes is warned by an uncle:

> 'You see how god strikes with his thunderbolt creatures that stand above the rest and removes them from his sight, but the small ones do not provoke him. You see how he is forever hurling his bolts upon the highest buildings and the tallest trees. For god loves to cut down all things that stand above the rest. So also in the case of a great army: it is destroyed by a small one whenever god in his jealousy makes it fearful or thunderstruck, whereby it perishes unworthily. For god suffers pride in none but himself.'
> (T.J. Luce, *The Greek Historians*, Routledge, 1997)

All too true: but it makes no difference to Xerxes' plans, and the inevitable disaster follows. In this respect Herodotus and the tragedian Sophocles share many of the same instincts.

6. Herodotus

Herodotus is unmatchable: endlessly curious, full of wonder, amusing and amused, humane, sceptical, open-minded, compassionate, a brilliant stylist and a truly great story-teller. Open his *Histories* anywhere and if your eyes are not popping out on stalks after two minutes, claim your money back.

The translations

Aubrey de Selincourt's Penguin translation has done noble service, and was revised with an excellent new introduction in 1996 (first-rate index too). George Rawlinson's venerable translation has a wonderful sonority to it. Godley's Loeb (with facing page Greek) is perfectly serviceable if somewhat pompous. Luce's is not a complete translation but a book about the Greek historians in general, with well translated examples. Waterfield's translation and introduction are both very good.

7

Thucydides

The most famous speech in the ancient world is Pericles' 'Funeral speech', celebrating the greatness of fifth-century BC Athens. Here is an extract:

> Let me say that our system of government does not copy the institutions of our neighbours. It is more the case of our being a model to others, than of imitating anyone else. Our constitution is called a democracy because power is in the hands not of a minority but of the whole people. When it is a question of settling private disputes, everyone is equal before the law; when it is a question of putting one person before another in positions of public responsibility, what counts is not membership of a particular class, but the actual ability which a man possesses. No one, so long as he has it in him to be of service to the state, is kept in political obscurity because of poverty ...
>
> Our love of what is beautiful does not lead to extravagance; our love of things of the mind does not make us soft. We regard wealth as something to be properly used, rather than as something to boast about. As for poverty, no one need be ashamed to admit it; the real shame is in not taking practical measures to escape from it.
>
> (Rex Warner, *Thucydides: The Peloponnesian War*, Penguin, 1972)

It is called the Funeral speech because it was delivered by the charismatic Athenian leader Pericles in 431 BC in honour of the Athenians who had been killed during the first year of the war against Sparta. This 'Peloponnesian War', as we call it (Thucydides did not call his work by that or any other name), was to become a twenty-seven-year battle for

54

supremacy between the two most powerful Greek city-states of the time – and was to end in 404 BC with Athens' defeat.

So far, so good. But how do we know about the speech? Only because it was reported by the historian of the war, the Athenian Thucydides (Greek *Thoukudides*, *c.* 460-400 BC). But how could he remember it? There were no tape-recorders or published transcripts in those days. Besides, Thucydides' history is full of speeches, many of which he could not possibly have heard. Is it really Thucydides' Funeral speech, and not Pericles' at all?

It is a difficult question. But Thucydides is, arguably, the first real historian, and he knows the historian's first duty is to describe his method of working. So he tells us how he constructed his speeches:

> With reference to the speeches in this history, some were deliv-
> ered before the war began, others while it was going on; some I
> heard myself, others I got from various quarters; it was in all cases
> difficult to carry them word for word in one's memory, so my
> habit has been to make the speakers say what was in my opinion
> demanded of them by the various occasions, of course adhering as
> closely as possible to the general sense of what they really said.
> (Richard Crawley, *Thucydides: The History of the Peloponnesian
> War*, Wordsworth Classics, 1997)

So Thucydides comes clean about his practice: at the very worst, he has tried to ensure that the speeches contain nothing incompatible with what was actually said. But we would still love to know – how much of Pericles' funeral speech is really Thucydides?

Thucydides is equally open about his information-gathering:

> As to the facts of the occurrences in the war, I have thought it my
> duty to give them, not as ascertained from any chance informant,
> nor as seemed to me probable, but only after investigating with
> the greatest possible accuracy each detail, in the case both of the
> events in which I myself participated and of those regarding which
> I got information from others.
> (C.F. Smith, *Thucydides* I, Loeb Classical Library no. 108, 1928)

And he goes on to say what problems this caused, because different people gave different accounts, out of partiality or lapses of memory.

This passion for accuracy set the standard for all future historians. Thucydides' influence in other areas too was to be immense. History for him, unlike Herodotus (whom he dismisses as 'mere romance'), was about war and politics and nothing else, a model that has dominated western historical writing ever since. So he hardly mentions anything about e.g. marriage, the family, economics, or the cultural and intellectual world. For example, women bulk large in Herodotus, *gunê* 'woman' occurring 373 times; in Thucydides the word occurs fewer than fifty times, the majority of those as 'children and women' (and usually in that order). Thucydides can seem austere at times.

Then again, Thucydides described events year-by-year, setting what was to become a popular precedent. Another major breakthrough (and typical of ancient Greeks) was his absolute exclusion of divine intervention (though he is, of course, well aware that others may be religiously motivated). If there is a down side, Thucydides offers no alternative versions of events (unlike Herodotus) and rarely quotes his sources. But one can hardly blame him for thinking he had reached 'the truth'.

That said, Thucydides' debt to Herodotus is obvious. Like Herodotus, Thucydides wants to interpret and explain as well as record contemporary events; like Herodotus, he ranges far and wide over the Greek-speaking world (the fact that Thucydides was exiled by the Athenians as a military commander in 424 BC for failing to carry out their orders left him free to move around); and like Herodotus, he has an eye and an ear for the powerful, dramatic scene . Here is his famous description of the departure of the Athenian army from Syracuse in 413 BC after the defeat of its fleet in the harbour:

The situation was appalling in every way: they were retreating after having lost all their ships, and instead of realising their grand expectations, they had put themselves and their very city in peril. As they abandoned the camp, there was something to inflict pain on the sight, the mind, of each and every man. For the dead were unburied, and whenever a soldier saw the body of a friend lying on the ground, he was filled with grief and terror. The sick and wounded, who were being left behind still alive, distressed the able-bodied more than those who had perished and seemed more pitiful than the dead. These men resorted to pleading and wailing, mortifying the others as they insisted on being taken along, and

56

calling out, one by one, to any friend or relative they saw. As the buddies they had shared the tents with were leaving, they would hang on them and follow them as far as they could, and when the strength in their bodies failed them, many sobbed and called the gods to witness as they were being abandoned. The whole army was so filled with tears and desperation that they could hardly get going, even though they were leaving enemy territory and what they had already suffered was beyond tears as they dreaded sufferings yet unknown. And still with downcast eyes they loathed themselves. they looked like nothing so much as a people fleeing a starved-out city, and a large one at that.
(Walter Blanco, *The Peloponnesian War*, Norton, 1998)

But it is Thucydides' powers of political analysis and insights into human nature that bear the most obvious mark of his genius. Here he observes how, in the course of a revolution on Corcyra (Corfu) in 427 BC, words change their meaning when ideologies are at work:

So civil war spread among the cities, and those which caught it later, hearing of what had happened before, went to far greater extremes in their new forms of ingenuity, both in the exquisiteness of what they attempted and in the outlandishness of the revenge they took. The words normally used to evaluate deeds were changed to fit what was thought justified. Irrational daring came to be regarded as loyal courage, and prudent hesitation a respectable cover for cowardice; restraint was deemed a pretext for lack of courage, and intelligence for everything meant not being active for anything.
(Peter Rhodes, *Thucydides: History III*, Aris and Phillips, 1994)

Here, he reports a debate between representatives of the island of Melos and an Athenian embassy in 416 BC. The Athenians have come to inform the Melians that they cannot remain neutral in the war between Athens and Sparta. If they try, the Athenians will destroy them.

Athenians: We recommend that you should try to get what it is possible for you to get, taking into consideration what we both really do think; since you know as well as we do that, when matters are discussed by practical people, the standard of justice depends on the equality of power to compel, and that in fact the strong do what they have the power to do and the weak accept what they have to accept.

Melians: Then in our view it is at any rate useful that you should not destroy a principle that is to the general good of all men – namely, that in the case of all who fall into danger there should be such a thing as fair play and just dealing ... this is a principle which affects you as much as anybody, since your own fall would be visited by the most terrible vengeance and would be an example to the world ...

Athenians: ... Our opinion of the gods and knowledge of men lead us to conclude that it is the general and necessary law of nature to rule wherever one can. This is not a law we made ourselves, nor were we the first to act upon it when it was made. We found it already in existence, and we shall leave it to exist for ever among those who come after us. We are merely acting in accordance with it, and we know that you or anybody else with the same power as ours would be acting in precisely the same way.

(Warner)

Here is the cynicism of power writ large. The Melians' pleas fell on deaf ears. The island was blockaded and surrendered. Adult males were put to death, the women and children sold into slavery.

Thucydides said that he composed his history as 'a possession for all time'. He believed, not that events came in cycles, but that situations similar to the Peloponnesian war would recur, and that his history would help people understand them. Perhaps. I should judge rather that no one can read Thucydides without better understanding themselves and the world of power politics.

The translations

Warner's translation is accurate and smooth but gives little impression of Thucydides' often abstract, somewhat tortured style. Crawley is better on this account. Smith (with facing-page Greek) aims for greater accuracy but is rather less easy to read. Blanco's translation aims for an accessible colloquiality. It has very useful essays and other material at the back. Rhodes, in an edition with facing-page Greek and an excellent commentary based on the translation (not on the Greek), comes out very well.

World's Classics will be publishing Benjamin Jowett's famous translation, revised by Simon Hornblower. Hornblower is writing a superb commentary on this revised translation (two vols. are already published, Books 1-3 and 4-5, Clarendon).

8

Euripides

Euripides is a tragedian (*c*. 485-406 BC), but we must begin with a comedy, *Frogs* by Aristophanes (406 BC). Dionysus, god of tragedy, is down in the underworld choosing a tragic poet to bring back to life. It's got to be Aeschylus (died *c*. 455 BC) or Euripides (died 406 BC), and a ludicrous literary contest is being staged to decide which. Aristophanes is looking for laughs, and this is the point: he knows precisely how to characterise Euripides to get a laugh. Euripides is a modern poet, and therefore rubbish. So he is accused of bringing on stage sex-mad women, talkative kitchen-sink characters uttering kitchen-sink senti-ments, many dressed in rags, depraved and (in short) a threat to Athenian morals. Dramatically, according to Aristophanes, Euripides is repetitive, frivolous and monotonous, and musically, inept. In fact, string him up.

This is all, good rollicking stuff. It is supposed to be. It is comedy. It is also, as a characterisation of Euripides' plays, tosh, though it has exerted a disproportionate influence that has blighted Euripides ever since. It is as if the assessment of a politician by a satirical magazine like *Private Eye* should be taken 2,500 years later as The Truth About That Politician, rather than as evidence for what *Private Eye* thought would make its readers laugh about her.

Let us therefore start with the great fourth-century polymath Aristotle. In his *Poetics*, he described Euripides as *tragikôtatos*, 'most able to arouse emotions'. Here Troy has fallen. Its men are dead, its women being taken off into slavery. The triumphant Greeks have decided to throw the baby son of the Trojan champion Hector off the battlements. The baby's mother Andromache has already been led off. It is left to the child's grandmother Hecuba (*Hekabe* in Greek) to receive the shattered little body, which is brought in on her son Hector's great shield:

8. Euripides

O little hands, sweet likeness of Hector's once,
now you lie broken at the wrists before my feet;
and mouth beloved, whose words were once so confident,
you are dead; and all was false, when you would lean across
my bed, and say: 'Grandma, when you die I will cut
my long hair in your memory, and at your grave
bring companies of boys my age, to sing farewell.'
It did not happen: now I, a homeless, childless old
woman must bury your poor corpse, which is so young.
Alas for all the tendernesses, my nursing care,
and all your slumbers gone.
(R. Lattimore in Grene and Lattimore (eds), *Euripides III*,
Chicago, 1958)

The detail and precision of Hecuba's description of her grandson's corpse are chilling, her refusal to gloss over the horrible reality, heroic. Women in Greek tragedy are frequently portrayed as the archetypes of suffering. Their men are dead: it is the women who have to endure slavery and exile, alone. Euripides returns again and again to explore female mentality and the sufferings of women.

Aristotle also said that Euripides portrayed 'men as they are'. Euripides was fascinated by the problems of what made people tick, and how the world worked. Athens in the fifth century BC was a-buzz with theories on these matters, and when Euripides wrote his tragedies, he infused traditional myths with this advanced thinking and questioning (hence Aristophanes' jibes).

Here, for example, Euripides makes the great hero Heracles question the old stories:

I do not believe that the gods acquiesce in illegitimate love and
have never thought them capable of chaining each other up. I shall
not believe that that one god is tyrant over another. A god if he is
truly god needs nothing. These are the miserable tales of poets.
(Shirley Barlow, *Euripides: Heracles*, Aris and Phillips, 1996)

Here, in his *Hippolytus*, Euripides explores the psychology of Phaedra, a woman desperately fighting against her feelings of lust for her stepson, and of Hippolytus, a stepson with a penchant for hunting, press-ups and cold

61

showers and a revulsion against women. Here Hippolytus has found out that Phaedra lusts after him:

> O Zeus, why did you allow women to live in the light of the sun and plague mankind with their counterfeit looks? If you wished to propagate the race of men, it wasn't from women you should have provided this; no, men ought to enter your temples and there purchase children at valuation, each at its appropriate price, depositing in exchange bronze or iron or weight of gold, and then live in freedom in their homes without women.
>
> (John Davie, *Euripides: Alcestis* etc., Penguin, 1996)

In *Medea*, Euripides stages a clash between Medea, a sorceress, and her husband Jason, who has decided to marry someone else. To punish her husband, Medea decides to kill their two sons. Here she contemplates what she is about to do:

> Such hope, I had such hopes of you:
> That you would care for me when I was old;
> When I died, your hands would wrap me for the grave –
> The final wish of man. Those dreams were sweet
> But they have come to nothing: bereft of you,
> I shall drag out a life of pain and grief,
> While you will never see your mother again
> With those dear eyes, but change into another life.
> My children, why are you staring at me so?
> Why do you smile at me, that last of all your smiles?
> What am I going to do? My heart gives way,
> It betrays me, when I see their shining faces,
> My babies. I cannot do it. Forget all plans
> I made before. I'll take my boys with me.
> How can I harm them just to hurt their father,
> When all his pain would be as nothing to mine?
> I will not do it. No. Goodbye, all my plans.
> What's happening to me? Do I really want
> To leave my enemies mocking me – and unpunished?
> I must be brave and do it. Coward woman,
> To let soft arguments invade my heart …
> Go, children; in; go in.
>
> (Alistair Elliot, *Euripides: Medea*, Oberon Books, 1993)

This lengthy internal debate sounds very up-to-date. One half expects the TV psychologist Dr Anthony Clare to lean forward and ask her whether she got on well with her mother.

'Modernity', however, is not confined to Euripides. There is in much Greek tragedy a sense of putting contemporary issues into the public arena via the world of heroic myth. To take an extreme example, Aeschylus' *Oresteia* reaches its climax with the foundation of the Areopagus, an ancient Athenian advisory body most of whose powers had recently been stripped from it by radicals in democratic Athens (it is extreme because it is so overtly political, and because the Areopagus and the Orestes' myth were unconnected until Aeschylus connected them). Here Creusa, having been reunited with Ion, her son from long ago by Apollo, hears Athene describe what Ion's part will be in shaping the Greek world (Xuthus is Creusa's husband):

> It is his right to rule my land [*Athens*]. He shall be famous throughout Greece ... (and his sons) shall colonize the lowlands on either side of the strait that divides Europe from Asia; called after this prince, they shall bear the glorious name of Ionians. Moreover, you and Xuthus too shall have sons: first Dorus, from whom shall spring the celebrate Dorian state; then Achaeus, who shall be king of the sea-coast by Rhium in the Peloponnese, and set the seal of his name upon the nation [*Achaeans*].
> (P. Vellacott, Euripides' *Ion* in *The Bacchae and Other Plays*, Penguin, 1973)

What did it mean to be an Athenian? Euripides has here reminded his audience of their heroic, divinely blessed origins, and how Ion's parents also helped shape the whole of the rest of the Greek world too. As the Athenians sat in the theatre, just under the magnificent Acropolis looming above them, they could see for themselves how powerful and glorious Ion's line had become, how much a mark of Apollo and Athene's divine favour, and how superior to other Greeks.

This leads to a second, equally vital point. Myth can bear any number of reinterpretations and re-workings. There is no such thing as a 'standard' version. For example, the myth of Orestes, Agamemnon's son, returning to take revenge for his father's death on his mother

Clytaemnestra is explored in completely different ways in Aeschylus *Libation Bearers*, and Sophocles' and Euripides' *Electra*s. In Aeschylus, Electra (Orestes' unmarried, despairing sister) plays no part in the palace killing; in Sophocles, she is the bitter, fixated driving force behind it; in Euripides, she has been married off to a virtuous peasant and lures her mother out to her hut under the pretence of having given birth, where Orestes slaughters her. The faintly suspicious Clytaemnestra enters, magnificently dressed – a condition Electra makes chilling reference to as she enters the house, because a sacrificial victim had to be unstained:

> *Clytaemnestra*: Why did you summon me, child?
> *Electra*: You heard, I think, that I had given birth; I want you to make the thanks offering, for I don't know how – whatever the custom prescribes for the baby's tenth day. I have never had a child before; I have no experience what to do.
> *Clytaemnestra*: This is the task of someone else, the woman who delivered you.
> *Electra*: I had no midwife; I had my baby without help.
> *Clytaemnestra*: Is your house so far from neighbours that could lend a helping hand?
> *Electra*: No one wants poor people as friends.
> *Clytaemnestra*: But look how dirty you are, how shabbily dressed for a woman who has only just given birth to a child! I will go inside to offer sacrifice for the child's tenth day ...
> *Electra*: Then enter my humble home; do please take care that your clothing isn't stained by all the smoke inside the cottage when you offer up the kind of sacrifice you must to the gods. [*Clytaemnestra disappears.*] The basket has been duly prepared for the rite and the knife whetted that felled the bull [*Agamemnon*]; next to it you will receive your own blow and fall!
> (John Davie, *Euripides: Electra and Other Plays*, Penguin, 1998)

In other words, when Athenian audiences took their seats for the dramatic festival of plays (two a year, in January and April) they expected something far more than a simple, traditional re-run of their Favourite, Hottest Myths.

While all the tragedians were experimentalists to some extent, Euripides in particular pushes the idea of what might be called tragedy to its limits. Some of his plays, with their exciting chases and dramatic, last-gasp revelations of true identity (like *Ion* above), seem more akin to melodrama. Here Menelaus, returning from Troy with his wife (in fact a wraith of his wife), has been shipwrecked in Egypt – where he will find his real wife has been all along (see the chapter on Herodotus, p. 47). He knocks on the door of the palace:

> *Old Woman*: Who is at our gates? You'ld better get away from the palace. Don't stand at our front gates and annoy our master with your uproar. Otherwise you'll be executed as a Greek – they have no business here.
> *Menelaus*: Old woman, you might use politer language. For I shall do what you say. Don't be so angry.
> *Old Woman*: Off with you! For it is my task, stranger, to make sure that no Greek approaches the palace.
> *Menelaus*: Ah, don't wave your fist at me and drive me away by force.
> *Old Woman*: It's your fault, for you are not doing as I tell you.
> *Menelaus*: Announce to your master inside ...
> *Old Woman*: I think that I would rue it if I delivered a message from you.
> *Menelaus*: I have come here a shipwrecked stranger – such men are guaranteed protection.
> *Old Woman*: Then go off to some other house and don't stay here.
> *Menelaus*: No, I shall come inside. And you, do what I say.
> *Old Woman*: You're being a nuisance, I tell you, and soon you'll get driven off forcibly.
> *Menelaus*: Alas, where is my glorious army?
> (James Morwood, *Helen*, in *Euripides: Medea, Hippolytus, Electra, Helen*, World's Classics, 1997)

Tragedies are serious business. But this is almost comic as (we are told) Menelaus, great husband of Helen, comes in covered with bits and pieces of flotsam from the wreck and engages in a knocking-at-the-door scene, almost entirely absent from tragedy but frequent in comedy. Menelaus eventually gets into the palace, finds out the truth about his real wife and is reunited with her. She, however, is being retained against her will by the king who wants to marry her. They manage to escape after conjuring up a trick about a 'funeral at sea for the dead Menelaus'. And that is a tragedy? It is certainly Euripides.

Euripides' most famous tragedy is his last, *Bacchae*. A bacchant is a female worshipper of the god Dionysus (also called Bacchus), and in this play Dionysus, disguised as a mortal, comes with his band of bacchants to establish his worship in Thebes. But the prim, fastidious young king Pentheus resists him. Eventually Dionysus takes control of him and persuades him to disguise himself as a bacchant so that he can spy on the women. Dionysus then reveals who he is and the enraged bacchants (among them his mother Agaue) uproot the tree where he is hiding:

> Then from his high perch plunging, crashing
> To the earth Pentheus fell, with one incessant scream
> As he understood what end was near. His mother first,
> As priestess, led the rite of death, and fell upon him.
> He tore the headband from his hair, that his wretched mother
> Might recognise him and not kill him. 'Mother', he cried,
> Touching her cheek, 'It is I, your own son Pentheus, whom
> You bore to Echion. Mother have mercy; I have sinned,
> But I am still your own son. Do not take my life!'
> Agaue was foaming at the mouth; her rolling eyes
> Were wild; she was not in her right mind, but possessed
> By Bacchus, and she paid no heed to him.
> (P. Vellacott, *Euripides: The Bacchae and Other Plays*)

He is torn to pieces and his mother, imagining she has been in a lion hunt, triumphantly bears his head back to the palace – where the truth is revealed.

This examination of a god's power to alter states of mind and perceptions, and of the ruthlessness with which the god hunts humans down, is open to all sorts of interpretation. One popular one has been that there is Dionysus in all of us; repress that god/instinct, and it will destroy us. All very sixties, man (when it was propounded). But in Euripides, most of all the tragedians, we are likely to find issues which can be easily – perhaps too easily – classified in our terms as 'feminist' or 'pacifist' or 'anti-religious' or 'psychological', and this is why he seems so strikingly modern.

The translations

Lattimore's *Trojan Women* is in the fine Chicago 'Complete Greek Tragedies' series (nine volumes in all). Barlow's accurate *Heracles* is in the Aris and Phillips series, with facing page Greek and commentary on the translation. Alistair Elliot's brilliantly actable *Medea* (Oberon) was produced for Diana Rigg. Vellacott has produced readable versions of all Euripides for Penguin. These are now being added to by John Davie's more accurate translations. World's Classics' new Euripides series by James Morwood stays as close to the Greek as possible.

'Actors of Dionysus' have produced their own version of *Medea* for Penguin Audiobooks (1997).

9

Aristophanes

Lysistrata is furious. She has summoned the women to an early-morning meeting, and no one has turned up. Eventually her neighbour Calonice arrives:

Cal: OK, Lysistrata, suppose
You tell me why we're meeting here. The deal.
Is it a big one?
Lys: Very big.
Cal: Not hard as well?
Lys: It's very hard.
Cal: Then why aren't we all here?
Lys: No, no, not that: if it were that, they'd come.
It's something I've been thinking hard about:
On sleepless nights I've tossed it back and forth.
Cal: I guess it must be pretty limp by now.
(Jeffrey Henderson, *Aristophanes' Lysistrata*, Focus Classical Library (USA), 1988)

This is the opening of Aristophanes' most famous comedy – *Lysistrata* (411 BC), where Lysistrata ('army-disbander') persuades the obviously sex-mad women (the single *entendres* of the opening lines above are typical) to call a sex-strike. After twenty years of war against Sparta, she has decided enough is enough – family life is being ruined. Not, of course, that having a sex-strike when the men are away at the war all the time makes a lot of sense, but who cares? This is Aristophanes (*c.* 450-386 BC).

Lysistrata follows a pattern common to Aristophanes' comedies. The hero is an insignificant person (here a woman, even!), who has some grand scheme to change the world. After the introductory scenes, the 24-strong Chorus enters, usually in opposition. A contest ensues which

69

our hero(ine) duly wins, the great reform is enacted, and the play ends in triumph. So Lysistrata persuades the women of all Greece to join her, captures the Acropolis of Athens (home of the state treasury), defeats the male Chorus and reduces both sides to begging her to make peace.

Fantasy lies at the heart of Aristophanes. When, for example, the ambassadors from Athens and Sparta come to make peace under Lysistrata's stern eye, they both sport vast erections (all male characters in comedy wore phalluses of variegated size and hue). The Chorus leader begins:

> *Leader*: Do tell us what has brought you here today.
> *Spartan*: What need is there for lengthy explanations?
> You see precisely what has brought us here.
> *Leader*: Phew! Yes, a tense condition you're suffering from!
> I see that matters now are worse inflamed.
> *Spartan*: Incredibly. The facts speak for themselves.
> We badly need an offer of terms for peace ...
> [*The Athenians enter in the same state.*]
> *Leader*: I diagnose a case of grave tumescence.
> *Athenian*: We need to find Lysistrata at once.
> The plight we're in is plain for all to see.
> *Leader*: This sickness is a perfect match for [*points to Spartan*] that.
> D'you find distension most acute at dawn?
> *Athenian*: Not half!
> (Stephen Halliwell, *Aristophanes: Birds* etc., Oxford, 1997)

The fact that even the most frustrated male does not actually walk about thus encumbered is quite irrelevant.

Here in *Peace* (421 BC) the little farmer Trygaeus sets off to heaven on a dung-beetle. He intends to demand that the gods send Peace back to earth, and he appeals to the audience:

> *Tryg*: Please, everybody – I'm doing all this for your sake – could you possibly abstain from shitting and farting for the next three days? If Pegasus here gets a whiff, he'll chuck me head over heels and swoop down for a meal! [*Sings*]:
> Come Pegasus, go on with joy,
>   Behind thee put all fears,
> Let golden-bridled harness sounds

Assail thy shining ears.
[*The beetle suddenly stops moving and assumes a descending attitude.*]
What doest thou? Why thus incline
     Thy nose towards the john?
Stretch forth thy wings in speedy flight,
     Away from earth! Go on! ...
Hey, you there in Peiraeus [*harbour of Athens*], where
     The whores and pimps abound!
What are you playing at, laying eggs
     Of shit upon the ground? ...
[*The beetle wobbles violently and Trygaeus all but falls off.*]
Heeeeelp! No, I mean, this is serious! Hey, you down there, the crane-handler, do for heaven's sake be a bit more careful!
(David Barrett and Alan Sommerstein, *Aristophanes: The Knights*, etc., Penguin, 1978)

The scheme, of course, is simply absurd, but that's Aristophanes. There's a lot more that is Aristophanic too in this extract. Pegasus was the famous horse that reached heaven – a fine parodic name for a dung-beetle. Observe too how Aristophanes varies the register of Trygaeus' words: from the coarse, to the (sung) lyrical, to tragic parody ('thou' and 'thy' on the heroic subject of lavatories). Is Aristophanes obscene? Certainly: but he is out in the open about it, before a huge audience. This is the opposite of pornographic.

Observe that Trygaeus also refers directly to the audience and even to the crane-handler behind the stage who would have been hoisting him up to 'heaven'. Greek tragedy never does this, but Aristophanes refers directly to the audience and stage mechanics all the time (this phenomenon is called 'metatheatre' and is always greeted with keen nodding by scholars).

But there is more to Aristophanes than little people. The well-known in Athens are parodied, insulted and ridiculed too. Here in *Clouds* (423 BC) the famous philosopher Socrates is roughed up. The foolish old man Strepsiades (an invented character) has come to Socrates' 'Reflectory' to find out how he can escape his debts. The place is full of reverential students of the Great Man. When Socrates finally appears, he is in a wicker cage, but suspended in the air (like a god). Strepsiades is filled with awe:

Streps: Socrates! My sweet little Socrates!
Soc: Why dost thou call me, thou creature of a day?
Streps: First of all, I beg you, tell me what you're doing.
Soc: I walk the air and descry the sun.
Streps: You mean you decry [*sic*] the gods from a wicker cage? Why not do it on the ground, if at all?
Soc: I could never have made correct discoveries about celestial phenomena except by hanging up my mind and mixing the minute particles of my thought into the air which it resembles. If I had been on the ground and investigated the upper regions from below, I would never have made my discoveries; for it is certain that the earth forcibly draws the moisture of thought to itself. Just the same thing happens to cress.
Streps: How do you mean? Thought draws moisture to cress?
(Alan Sommerstein, *The Comedies of Aristophanes, vol. 2: Clouds*, Aris and Phillips, 1982)

The whole point about Socrates is that he had no interest in how the world worked (unlike many Greek thinkers): he was interested in how men should best lead their lives (see Chapter 10). That makes no difference to Aristophanes. Socrates is parodied as if he were a divine being and then as a stereotype 'intellectual', and made to talk the sort of pompous, incomprehensible, 'scientific' twaddle that the average Athenian man-in-the-audience thought intellectuals talked (and to which Strepsiades reacts accordingly). Intellectuals were favourite targets for popular abuse. We saw in the last chapter that the 'intellectual' tragic playwright Euripides was always being ridiculed by comedians.

But did the Athenians get all these intellectual jokes? *Frogs*, for example (see the start of the chapter on Euripides, p. 60), reaches its climax in a literary contest, overseen by the god of drama Dionysus, between Aeschylus and Euripides, who hurl lines from their work at each other – in Aeschylus' case, first written over fifty years earlier. Here Dionysus prepares to 'weigh' their verses 'like cheese'. The two poets are invited to speak a verse into the pans of a weighing scale and when Dionysus gives the word, let the pan go:

Dionysus: Right, take hold.
Euripides: }Ready!
Aeschylus: }

9. Aristophanes

Dionysus: Fire away, then.

Euripides: 'No temple hath Persuasion, save in words.'

Aeschylus: 'Alone of all the gods, Death takes no gifts.'

Dionysus: Let go. Now, let's see. It's this one. You see, he put in Death. That's a heavy word if you like.

Euripides: Well, what about Persuasion, doesn't that carry any weight? A beautiful line, too.

Dionysus: No, Persuasion won't do: mere empty words without sense. You'll have to think of something really ponderous, to weigh your side down. Something strong and big.

Euripides: What have I got that's strong and big? Umm, let me think.

Dionysus: What about that stirring line 'Achilles threw two singles and a four'? Well, come on now, this is the last round.

Euripides: 'He seized his mighty bludgeon, ribbed with iron.'

Aeschylus: 'Chariot on chariot, corpse on corpse was piled.'

Dionysus: He's licked you again.

Euripides: I don't see why.

Dionysus: All those chariots and corpses – a hundred Egyptians couldn't lift that lot.

(D. Barrett, *Aristophanes: The Wasps*, etc., Penguin, 1964)

It is at once clear how Aristophanes has played it. The joke is self-explanatory – or is explained for you – whether you know the lines or not. Even if the joke is not obvious, it is still easy to signify 'poetic line' and trigger a laugh if the actor adopts an appropriate voice or gesture when saying it (not expression – actors wore masks in the ancient world). The audience, in other words, is helped through the quotation by the playwright – while those who get the reference anyway are left feeling smugly superior.

Aristophanes' plots are contemporary, reflecting some mood or trend in Athens. They often arise from the political situation (the plays about peace, for example) and living politicians and soldiers are as viciously vilified as anyone. Here a foul-mouthed invented character Sausage-Seller and the living politician Cleon (thinly disguised as a Paphlagonian, a barbarian slave from Asia Minor), both yearning for power, compete to show how much they love old Demos (Thepeople):

73

Paph: ... I promise to provide you with a whole bowlful of jury pay to guzzle every day, and you needn't do anything at all!
SS: I'll give you a little box with ointment in, so you can soothe the sores on your leg!
Paph: I'll pluck out your grey hairs and make you young again!
SS: Look, take this hare's tail to wipe your eyes with!
Paph: Blow your nose, Thepeople, and use my head to wipe your hands!
SS: No, use mine!
Paph: No, mine!
(Barrett and Sommerstein, *The Knights*)

There is much argument about whether Aristophanes was intending to make a serious contribution, through humour, to the political debate. I think not. I doubt that *Yes, Minister*, *Private Eye* or *Spitting Image*, for example, have ever persuaded anyone to change their political allegiance. Comedy is not an effective medium for political intervention, however 'political' its subject matter. Even Aristophanes' plays about peace offer no specific programme for its negotiation. They imagine, longingly, a fantasy situation in which war has ended – a longing doubtless shared by all Athenians. But peace cannot just be 'declared' – or rather, it can be 'declared' only by comedians. Few people during the Second World War, for example, would have opted for peace with Hitler's Germany on any terms, however much they longed for it. Besides, the Athenian Assembly of all Athenian males over 18 met every 8 days to make all the decisions about Athens that our government makes for us. A single comedy put on once in competition, like tragedy, at a dramatic festival is an unlikely engine for serious debate.

What Aristophanes is all about is making Athenians laugh. He does this primarily by constructing plots that appeal to the audience's desire to get their own back on those who are stronger or better than they are – gods, politicians, intellectuals, artists, generals, officials, whoever – by all verbal and visual means possible, no holds barred. Like all serious humorists, he directs his bolts not at the system (he never criticises the democracy) but mainly at individuals operating the system.

But perhaps the greatest miracle of all is Aristophanes' stunningly inventive use of language. He wields a vast vocabulary, and brings unparalleled imagination to bear on it. Here are some of his words for the male organ: tip, eel, meat, skin, finger, equipment, thing, muscle, dried fig, fig-petals, mallow stalk, acorn, chickpea, barleycorn, spear, pole, peg, ram, oar, goad, beam, bolt, handle, spit-roast, axe, club, staff, top, token, drill, thong, wing, tail, sparrow, foot, rope, lump, soup-ladle. And for the female: box, piggie, sucking pig, fig, pomegranate, myrtle berry, rose, garden, meadow, thicket, grove, plain, celery, mint, fuzz, door, gate, sheath, ring, circle, hole, cave, pit, gulf, hollow, vent-hole, sea-urchin, hearth, brazier, hot coals, bowl, dish, boiled sausage, barley cake, pancake, nightingale, thrush, mouse-hole, bird's nest, swallow, gravy-boat.

Beat that.

To end this chapter with a proviso. Both Aristophanic comedy and Greek tragedy are sophisticated and popular art-forms, going on tour to local festivals after their performance in Athens. But there were other forms of popular drama too – especially mime (and for the Romans, pantomime) – whose 'stars' could make a fortune.

Such performances, put on by males and females, could include song-and-dance routines, schmaltzy melodrama (we hear of Greek heroines being rescued from Indian courts), explicit sexual escapades (how the wife poisoned her husband so that she could have it off with the slaves), and so on. We could make the same mistake about western culture if in 3,000 years time we were to give the impression that the Royal Shakespeare Company was the people's only idea of fun today, forgetting entirely about TV.

The reason why we know so little about such performances is that texts of them do not survive. In the eyes of those who made decisions about what was worth preserving (e.g. scholars and schoolmasters), they were low art, with no uplifting messages to convey, unworthy of transmission to future generations.

The translations

Henderson's racy, modernised American translation whizzes along. Halliwell's, the first volume of the World's Classics series, is more accurate and has full essays and notes. Barret and Sommerstein, with an eye on easy, witty readability, have translated all Aristophanes for Penguin (three volumes). Sommerstein's excellent play-by-play Aris and Phillips' editions of Aristophanes offer facing-page Greek text and enlightening commentary on the translation.

10

Socrates and Plato

Anaximander of Miletus (*c.* 610-540 BC) says he thinks that from hot water and earth there arose fish, or animals very like fish, that humans grew in them, and that the embryos were retained inside up to puberty whereupon the fish-like animals burst and men and women emerged already able to look after themselves.
(Censorinus, in J. Barnes, *Early Greek Philosophy*, Penguin, 1987)

Eternity is a child at play, playing draughts; the kingdom is a child's.
(Heraclitus, *c.* 500 BC, in Barnes)

The first western philosophers like Anaximander and the amazing Heraclitus (seventh-fifth century BC) were primarily concerned with questions about where the universe came from, what its nature and basic substance were, and how it worked.

Having hardly any concept of experiment and lacking anything remotely resembling scientific procedures and the technology that makes them possible (those awaited the eighteenth century AD), all they could do was observe the external world and draw conclusions. But they believed the world was rational and could therefore be apprehended by reason; they rejected supernatural explanations of its origins and development; and finally, all their conclusions were regarded as open to dispute. There were no higher authorities (e.g. priest castes) looking to suppress debate (perhaps one of the keys to the Greek achievement). All this qualifies these Greeks as the first true philosophers of the west, and lifts the curtain on a frame of mind – strongly independent, willing to debate anything with anyone – that goes some way to explaining the Greek intellectual achievement.

These philosophers are lumped together under the title of 'the Presocratics' because the advent of Socrates (469-399 BC) tilted the balance of the debate away from the natural world to the study of human beings. Socrates asked not 'where do we come from?' but 'how can we best lead our lives?'

Socrates' starting point was the typically paradoxical claim that ignorance was the beginning of wisdom. Here, on trial for his life in 399 BC, he explains to the jury in his defence speech (*apologia*) how he reached that conclusion. A friend, he says, had asked the oracle at Delphi if there was anyone wiser than Socrates. To Socrates' absolute amazement, the oracle had answered 'no':

> When I heard about the oracle's answer, I said to myself 'What is the god saying, and what is his hidden meaning? I am only too conscious that I have no claim to wisdom, great or small; so what can he mean by asserting that I am the wisest man in the world? He cannot be telling a lie; that would not be right for him.'
>
> After puzzling about it for some time, I set myself at last with considerable reluctance to check the truth of it in the following way. I went to interview a man with a high reputation for wisdom, because I felt that here if anywhere I should succeed in disproving the oracle and pointing out to my divine authority, 'You said that I was the wisest man, but here is a man who is wiser than I am.'
>
> Well, I gave a thorough examination to this person – I need not mention his name, but it was one of our politicians that I was studying when I had this experience – and in conversation with him I formed the impression that although in many people's opinion, and especially in his own, he appeared to be wise, in fact he was not. Then when I began to try to show him that he only thought he was wise and was not really so, my efforts were resented both by him and by many of the other people present. However, I reflected as I walked away: 'Well, I am certainly wiser than this man. It is only too likely that neither of us has any knowledge to boast of; but he thinks that he knows something which he does not know, whereas I am quite conscious of my ignorance. At any rate it seems that I am wiser than he is to this small extent, that I do not think that I know what I do not know.'
> (H. Treddenick and H. Tarrant, 'The Apology', in *The Last Days of Socrates*, 1993, Penguin)

For Socrates, 'the unexamined life is not worth living'.

Socrates thought a life of goodness alone brought happiness, and if we only knew what goodness was, we would automatically do it, because everyone wanted to be happy (hence two further Socratic paradoxes – 'goodness is knowledge' and 'no one errs intentionally'). So we had better define what goodness was. Then we would recognise it and act accordingly. He proceeded by a process of question-and-answer (dialectic, cf. dialogue) – a technique he invented. To illustrate it, Socrates is here trying to get Polemarchus to define morality:

S: So morality is doing good to one's friends and harm to one's enemies?

P: I think so.

S: Now, where sickness and health are concerned, who is best able to do good to his friends and harm to his enemies when they aren't well?

P: A doctor.

S: And where the risks of a sea voyage are concerned, when friends are on board ship?

P: A ship's captain.

S: And what about a moral person? In which walk of life or for what activity is he best able to benefit his friends and harm his enemies?

P: In fighting against enemies and in support of friends, I'd say.

S: All right. Now, my dear Polemarchus, a doctor is no use unless people are ill.

P: True.

S: And a captain is no use unless people are on a sea voyage.

P: Quite so.

S: Is a moral person, then, no use to anyone who is not at war?

P: No, I don't agree with that.

S: So morality is useful during times of peace too?

P: Yes.

S: And so is farming. Yes?

P: Yes.

S: To provide us with crops?

P: Yes.

S: And shoe making too?

P: Yes.

S: To provide us with shoes?

P: Exactly.

S: All right, then. What can we use morality for? What does it provide us with?
(R. Waterfield, *Plato: Republic*, World's Classics, 1993)

Observe three very important features of Socrates' method here. First, he works by analogy – that is, by comparison – with the technical arts. As there are skills of doctoring and sailing and farming and shoemaking, so there is a skill of morality. Which does not mean we should not ask – is there? Are these things all comparable? Is it really the case that moral problems and the language in which they are expressed are on the same sort of footing as technical ones?

Second, his questions show up where a person's thinking has gone wrong, but they offer that person a way out, a chance to redefine and rethink what he has been saying. Socrates rarely produces a definitive answer to any of his questions (he never defined that elusive 'goodness'). What he does do is make one realise one's ignorance – and so start thinking afresh.

Third, observe Socrates' fascination with definitions. Convinced as he was that 'goodness' could be defined with the same accuracy as a 'shoe', he devised a powerful method of definition. That is, he invited people to offer *individual* examples of 'goodness' to see if, once they were all put together, a general definition would emerge. So he might get his listeners to agree that standing up to the enemy in battle is 'good'; supporting one's aged parents is 'good'; disarming a violent man is 'good' – so what do those examples all have in common that makes them 'good'?

Socrates was too hot to handle. His radical questioning of everything seemed too threatening, and he also had some nasty friends who in 403 BC had destroyed Athenian democracy and briefly wielded bloody power before being dislodged. He was tried on charges of impiety and corrupting the young, found guilty, and executed. Here is the end of his defence speech, where he makes one final request of those who have condemned him to death:

It concerns my sons. If you think, gentlemen, when they grow up, that they are more interested in money – or anything else – than goodness, you must get your own back on them and make their lives a misery in exactly the same way I made yours a misery. If they think they are something when they are nothing, then reproach them as I reproached you. Tell them they are giving no thought to the things that matter, and that they think they are something when they are worth nothing. If you do this, I shall have been fairly treated by you myself, and so will my sons.

I must stop. It is time for us to go. Me to my death, you to your lives. Which of us goes to the better fate, only god knows.

(T. Griffith, 'Apology' in *Plato: Symposium and the death of Socrates*, Wordsworth Classics, 1997)

Socrates never wrote a word: his life and thought are recorded by his disciple Plato (429-347 BC: Plato is a nick-name, 'broad-shouldered' – his real name was Aristocles). Since Plato always uses Socrates as a mouthpiece, there is a great debate about where Socrates ends and Plato begins. But all Plato's work sprang from Socrates' concern with definitions, and he set up his famous Academy to pursue the issues in detail.

Plato essentially does two things. First, he tries to provide an answer to the problem – if we do not know what goodness is, how can we possibly start to define it? His answer is highly theoretical. Like Socrates, he starts from the physical. He points out that (for example) while we all know what a table is and can recognise one, we can still never give a definition that will cover every conceivable type of table that might ever exist. So how can we be said really to *know* what a table is? Plato insists that we recognise 'tableness' because somewhere 'out there' there in fact exists the idea, form or concept of the perfect table, which is grasped only by the soul. An earthly table is a table because it dimly reflects that unearthly, perfect table. So with 'goodness' – the perfected form or concept does exist, and this enables us to recognise pale shadows of it on earth. The education of the soul, which Plato sees as quite distinct from the body, will enable us to understand these concepts.

But how does Plato know the soul exists with the capabilities he wants of it? Here he abandons rational argument and at the end of the *Republic* turns to a story, his famous myth of Er. Er is a soldier who dies, witnesses what happens to the soul after death, and then, restored to life, reveals all, especially about the rewards and punishments that await the moral/just and immoral/unjust. The story begins:

Er said that, when he had left his body, his soul journeyed with a great crowd; and they came to a supernatural place in which there

80

were two chasms in the earth next to one another, and two others facing them up in the sky. Judges were seated between these, and after each judgement, they would instruct the just, after attaching to the front of them tokens of the verdict passed, to take the right-hand way up through the sky, and the unjust to take the lower left-hand way, after giving these too tokens on their back of all the deeds they had done.

(Stephen Halliwell, *Plato: Republic 10*, Aris and Phillips, 1988)

Second, Plato goes on to consider the social implications of his argument. If there is such a thing as 'absolute goodness' and men or women (Plato is very radical here) with the right training of the soul can aspire to it, then a state would be best run only by those who possess that special knowledge. Hence his famous theory of 'philosopher kings' – for only those with the proper philosophical training (devised, naturally, by Plato) will reach this knowledge and therefore have the right to rule:

> Unless communities have philosophers as kings, or the people who are currently called kings or rulers practise philosophy with complete integrity – in other words, unless political power and philosophy coincide, and all the people with their diversity of talents who currently head in different directions towards either government or philosophy have those doors shut firmly in their faces – there can be no end to political troubles, or even to human troubles in general.
>
> (Waterfield: *Plato: The Republic*)

Plato's famous *Republic* is an extended discussion of what a perfectly *dikaios* (just, moral) society would be like, with a view to establishing what a perfectly *dikaios* individual human should be like.

This sounds all very pie-in-the-sky, but Plato was serious about putting his beliefs into practice. He had a shot at realising his perfect society on earth when he was invited to the royal court of Dionysius II in Sicily. Alas for Plato, he found out that Dionysius was not quite so committed to Platonic ideals as he had hoped and the whole venture ended in an embarrassing shambles. Here in his famous *Seventh Letter* Plato describes his approach:

When I arrived [in Sicily] I made it my first task to discover whether Dionysius was genuinely on fire with enthusiasm for philosophy or whether the frequent reports to this effect which had come from Athens were baseless. There is a way of testing this which involves no loss of dignity and is quite suitable for absolute rulers, especially such as are full of second-hand ideas, which I perceived as soon as I arrived to be very much the case with Dionysius. The method is to demonstrate to such people the nature of the subject as a whole, and all the stages that must be gone through, and how much labour is required.

(Plato goes on to say that man who responds to this approach will follow it 'with all his might if life is to be worth living'.)

But those who are not genuinely lovers of wisdom, in whom philosophy is no more than a superficial veneer like the tan men get from exposing themselves to the sun, once they see how much there is to learn and how much labour is involved and the disciplined way of life that the subject requires, decide that the task is too hard for them and beyond their scope. They are not in fact fit to practise philosophy, though some of them persuade themselves that they have a sufficient grasp of the whole matter and need give themselves no further trouble about it. This then is the clearest and safest test to apply to those who like soft living and are incapable of hard work; it has the advantage that a man has only himself to blame if he cannot meet the demands of the subject, and his guide is absolved from responsibility.
(W. Hamilton, *Plato: Phaedrus and Letters VI and VII*, Penguin, 1973)

Dionysius did not come up to scratch, and Plato was reduced to turning his idealised *Republic* into a set of recommendations, which he wrote up in his last work, *The Laws*. Here, for example, Plato establishes the principles on which punishment will be inflicted:

When anyone commits an act of injustice, serious or trivial, the law will combine instruction and constraint, so that in future either the criminal will never again dare to commit such a crime involuntarily, or he will do it a very great deal less often; and in addition, he will pay compensation for the damage he has done. This is something we can achieve only by laws of the highest quality. We may take action or simply talk to the criminal; we may grant him pleasures or make him suffer; we may honour him, we may disgrace him; we can fine him or give him gifts. We may use absolutely any means to make him hate injustice and embrace true justice – or at any rate not hate it. But suppose the lawgiver finds a man who's beyond cure – what legal penalty will he provide for this case? He will recognise that the best thing for all such people is to cease to live – best even for themselves. By passing on they will help others too: first, they will constitute a warning against injustice, and secondly they will leave the state free of scoundrels. (T.J. Saunders, *Plato: The Laws*, Penguin, 1970)

Plato, then, is far more than a speculative philosopher: his theoretical beliefs about goodness and justice are used to underpin a practical vision of how society could best be organised. As with most ancient philosophers, Plato believed that philosophy should be *useful*.

The translations

Barnes' book surveys the founders of western philosophy. Penguin have translated most of Plato, pretty well on the whole. The Waterfield and Griffith are outstanding rivals. Halliwell's text with translation and commentary on the translation is excellent.

Socrates' *Apology* (defence speech) is the place to begin, then *Crito* (Socrates in prison) and *Phaedo* (the immortality of the soul, and Socrates' death). The *Republic* and *Symposium* (on the nature of love) – both pure Plato – are well worth reading.

11

Greek Epigrams

Rome conquered Greece in the second century BC. Though Greeks had been living in south Italy for centuries, it was this intensive contact with mainland Greek culture that really triggered Roman literature. But political control from Rome did not mean Greeks stopped either being Greek or producing Greek literature. Greek epigrams, as we shall see, were written throughout the Roman period.

To us an epigram is 'a short poem leading up to and ending in a witty or ingenious turn of thought' (*SOED*). To ancient Greeks, an epigram (*epigramma*) was originally an inscription (*epigramma* and Latin *inscriptio* both derive from words meaning 'write on'). These inscriptions were written on an object, in metre, saying who it belonged to, who dedicated it to what god, who made it, or who was buried underneath it.

The earliest example of Greek writing (*c.* 730 BC) is in fact an epigram, inscribed on a cup. It says 'I am the well-drunk drinking-cup of Nestor./Whoever drinks from this drinking cup, at once/Desire for fair-crowned Aphrodite will seize him.' This was composed (mostly) in hexameters (six feet to a line), but the metre for epigrams in Greek eventually settled down to become the elegiac couplet – the six-foot hexameter + five-foot pentameter. Translators have generally chosen not to try to represent this constricting medium.

The earliest surviving epigrams, like that on the cup, tend to be inscriptions carved on monuments. They are closely associated with their physical location. As a result, their range is restricted and they are anonymous, though many were ascribed to well-known writers by the ancients. The poet Simonides (*c.* 550-460 BC) is credited with the most famous of all, set up in Thermopylae in memory of the Spartans who fought the Persians there (480 BC), knowing it would be their death. The poet imagines a passer-by coming across it at the spot where they were killed:

Inform the Spartans we obeyed
Their orders, stranger. Here we stayed.
(Peter Hadley, *Epic to Epigram*, Bristol Classical Press, 1991)

But in the fifth and fourth centuries BC these inscriptions begin to be quoted in documents and so to lose their close association with their site: they become 'literature'. As a result, epigram stretches its wings and takes off in the post-classical, so-called Hellenistic period (320-30 BC). No longer confined to inscriptions in fixed locations, it becomes a poetic medium in its own right, and practitioners proudly put their names to their products. Big names emerge like Asclepiades, Callimachus, Meleager and Philodemus. Subjects now cover a huge range of topics, though death, lust and passion, wine, women and boys are constant favourites.

Here is an epigram by Callimachus (third century BC), famous for this translation by the Etonian schoolmaster, William Cory. Callimachus (who lived in Alexandria in Egypt) conjures up a picture of himself being brought the unexpected news of the death (years ago) of his old friend Heraclitus. Heraclitus lived in Caria (S.W. Turkey). Obviously, they had not seen each other for a long time. The 'nightingales' may be the title of a book of Heraclitus' poems:

They told me, Heraclitus, they told me you were dead;
They brought me bitter news to hear and bitter tears to shed.
I wept, as I remember'd, how often you and I
Had tired the sun with talking and sent him down the sky.

And now that thou art lying, my dear old Carian guest,
A handful of grey ashes, long long ago at rest,
Still are they pleasant voices, thy nightingales, awake,
For Death he taketh all away, but them he cannot take.
(A. Poole and J. Maule, *The Oxford Book of Classical Verse in Translation*, Oxford 1995)

Nightingales, of course, sing in the dark.

Here are some typical Hellenistic funerary epigrams, the one exploiting the poet's new opportunities to celebrate humble creatures (a dog), the others with a witty punch-line:

Stranger, commemorated here
   'Tis but a dog you see,
And yet, I beg you, do not sneer:
   My master wept for me

– Wept as the dusty earth he pressed
   Above my lifeless head,
And wrote, where now I lie at rest,
   The words that you have read.
(Anon.; Hadley)

I, Dionysus, lie here dead
And Tarsus was my native city.
In sixty years I never wed:
My father did – and more's the pity.
(Anon.; Hadley)

Remember Euboulos, who lived and died sober?
This is his grave. We might as well drink, then:
We'll all drop anchor in the same final harbour.
(Leonidas; by Fleur Adcock in *The Greek Anthology* (ed. P. Jay),
Penguin, 1981)

From death to serious matters, then: to sex. Like the Greek lyric poets
whom we have already looked at (p. 23ff.), epigrammatists tend to talk
not about love so much as lust and its powerful hold on them, their
hopes and fears and feelings when they dream of, gain or lose the objects
of their carnal desire. Eternal commitment never comes into it.

Here Meleager (*c.* 100 BC) gives instructions to a mosquito to take a
message to his beloved:

Buzz off and take a telegram for me, mosquito dear;
Go, settle on the tip of my Zenophila's sweet ear:
'Are you never, never coming?' (runs the song that you'll be
   humming)
'You're forgetting how he's fretting while you're slumbering up here.'

Fly away and make your music – ah, but softly, if you please
(Her husband mustn't wake and hear such messages as these),

And I promise, on condition you're successful in your mission,
I'll requite you, and this night you'll be a second Hercules.
(Hadley)

In the Greek Meleager wittily explains how the mosquito will become
'a second Hercules' – it will be presented with a club and lion-skin.

Greek males were happily bisexual. Here the same Meleager cele-
brates Alexis:

At 12 o'clock in the afternoon,
  In the middle of the street –
    Alexis

Summer had all but brought the fruit
  To its perilous end:
    & the summer sun and that boy's look

did their work on me.
  Night hide the sun.
    Your face consumes my dreams.

Others feel sleep as feathered rest;
  Mine but in flame refigures
    Your image lit in me.
(Peter Whigham in Jay)

These next two couplets are ascribed to the philosopher Plato, probably
wrongly. They are addressed to a beloved boy Aster, which means 'star':

My star, star-gazing? – If only I could be
The sky, with all those eyes to stare at you!

You were the morning star among the living:
But now in death your evening lights the dead.
(Peter Jay in Jay)

Here, Strato too (second century AD) dreams of love in somewhat
slushier mode:

11. Greek Epigrams

When Moeris said goodnight, she seemed to hold me
    And kiss my lips – and yet, for all I know,
I dreamed it. I remember all she told me
    And all I said to her, but I can show
It was a dream: for, if the kiss was given,
Why now am I on earth, and not in Heaven?
(Hadley)

For 'Moeris' write 'Kylie' and you have a Top Twenty hit on your hands.
This reminds one of 'Drink to me only' by Ben Jonson:

It is not wine that makes me reel
    Not juice of grape I crave,
Only to drink where you have drunk
    A wine no grape e'er gave.

Let but your lip the wine-cup lip
    Touch – how can I flee
Or wine or sweet cup-bearer, for
    The kiss it bears to thee?
(Agathias, *c.* AD 550, by Whigham, in Jay)

There are celebrations of the famous. Here the lecherous poet Anacreon
is remembered:

This is Anacreon's grave. Here lie
The shreds of that exuberant lust,
But hints of perfume linger by
His gravestone still, as if he must
Have chosen for his last retreat
A place perpetually on heat.
(Antipater, second century BC, by R. Skelton, in Jay)

There's satire too:

Wig, rouge, honey, wax, teeth:
With a make-up bill like yours
You'd save money buying a face.
(Lucilius, *c.* AD 60, by Peter Porter, in Jay)

Though a recent massive earthquake moved the earth, the skies,
   the lot,
Erasistratus the runner still stayed rooted to the spot.
(Lucilius, by Peter Jones, from the Greek of the Loeb *The Greek Anthology IV*, no. 85, Heinemann-Harvard, 1918)

With a face like that, Olympicus, you'd better never gaze
Upon yourself in spring or shining brook.
For, like Narcissus, once you've seen your face for what it's worth,
You'll hate yourself to death with every look.
(Lucilius, by Peter Jones, from Loeb)

There's bleak pessimism:

Born crying, and after crying, die.
It seems the life of man is one long cry.

Man, pitiful and weak and full of tears
Shows his face on earth, and disappears.
(Palladas, fourth century AD, by Tony Harrison, in Jay)

You name it, it's there. There's even a hymn in praise of grammar. The influence of these epigrams on Roman writers like the love-poet Catullus and the satirist Martial was to be enormous.

The translations

These epigrams survive by having been gathered together into *The Greek Anthology* in the tenth century AD. This is published in its entirety by Loeb (five vols., Greek and rather laboured facing-page translations). The Jay anthology in Penguin offers the most accessible and wide ranging selection of modern translations, while Poole and Maule, covering *all* classical literature, have a small selection of epigrams. Hadley's translations of the epigrams in his anthology of Latin and Greek verse strike me as very clever.

12

Plautus

Think Roman comedy, think Frankie Howerd, *Up Pompeii* and *A Funny Thing Happened on the Way to the Forum*. That is not quite all there is to say about Roman comedy, but it certainly sets the scene well enough. Now, adopt a Frankie Howerd face, posture and tone of voice, throw in the occasional 'oooo-eeer-aaaah yes/no', and off you go:

Pseudolus: You're very silent, master. If I could learn from your silence what troubles and torments are torturing your soul, I'd be glad to save us both trouble – me the trouble of asking and you the trouble of replying. But as that is impossible, I must needs put a few questions to you. Can you tell me, master, why you've been going round half-dead these last few days, and carrying that tablet with you everywhere, and soaking it with your tears, instead of finding someone to confide in? Come on, master, tell me. Let me into your secrets.
Calidorus: O Pseudolus, I am the most unhappy wretch alive.
Ps: Jupiter forbid it!
Cal: Jupiter has got nothing to do with it. I'm suffering under the tyranny of Venus, not Jupiter.
Ps: Won't you tell me all about it then? I've always been your chief privy counsellor up till now.
Cal: You still are.
Ps: Then tell me what the trouble is. Money, service, or advice, all I have is at your disposal.
Cal: Look at this letter, then, and see for yourself what kind of pain and misery is wasting my life away.
Ps: I will. Give it here … What – what in the world does this mean?
Cal: Why?
Ps: All these letters – they seem to be playing at mothers and fathers – crawling all over each other.

91

Cal: Oh, if you're going to make a joke of it –

Ps: It would take a Sibyl to read this gibberish; no one else could make head or tail of it.

Cal: Why are you so unkind to those dear little letters, written on that dear little tablet by that dear little hand?

Ps: A chicken's hand, was it? Some chicken surely scratched these marks.

(E.F. Watling, *Plautus: The Pot of Gold and Other Plays*, Penguin, 1965)

This is the opening of *Pseudolus*, one of Plautus' most brilliant comedies. Plautus deals essentially in types, and *Pseudolus* contains the usual basic plot and the usual basic cast: the love-sick young son, his old father who is determined to prevent him getting the girl, the girl herself, already sold by the pimp to a rich mercenary soldier, and the star of the show, the tricky, boastful, outrageous slave Pseudolus who, against all the odds, will win through and deliver the girl to the young master, fleecing the father of the necessary in order to do so.

Plautus was producing his comedies around 200 BC. They are the earliest Latin works to have survived complete. They also foreshadow a major feature of virtually all Latin literature – they look back to Greek literature as the primary source of inspiration (see p. 85). But it was not from the politicised, fantastic, obscene, absurd comic world of Aristophanes that Plautus took his cue. That sort of humour, 'old comedy', died with Athenian democracy. Plautus' plays were freely adapted from the later Greek 'new comedy' of Menander (*c.* 344-291 BC) – a semi-realistic, domestic world of youthful love-affairs, foundlings, twins and mistaken identities, and with a happy ending. But though Plautus' plays were performed in Greek dress, with Greek settings, names, costumes and masks, they were still utterly Roman and were hugely popular with Roman audiences.

Menander's plays are rich in subtle characters. Plautus takes them over and exaggerates them to suit the tastes of his Roman audience. Here the fantastically miserly Euclio, who is hiding a pot of gold and is terrified it will be stolen, has popped out of the house, leaving his old maidservant Staphyla in charge. He gives her strict orders to save the cobwebs, not light the fire (in case someone wants a light), say the well has run dry if anyone wants water, and all his kitchen utensils have been stolen if anyone wants them, and not even let Lady Luck in if she calls

(later a cook calls him so miserly that he sleeps with a bag over his mouth so as not to lose any breath, collects his fingernails when they've been clipped, and refuses to throw away his bath water). Outside Euclio meets a rich neighbour Megadorus who, quite ignorant of Euclio's money, wants to marry his daughter:

Meg: Are things as you would like them?
Eu: [*aside*] A trick – I sense a trick when rich men speak so
          lavishly to the poor.
          That fellow knows that I have gold. Why else would he be
          so polite?
Meg: Do I take it that you are well?
Eu: Uh – not financially.
Meg: But they say that if you're happy, that's money in the bank.
Eu: [*aside*] Damn – that hag's shown him the gold it's clearly clear.
          When I get home I'll cut her tongue out and gouge out
          her eyes!
Meg: Talking to yourself?
Eu: Uh yes, bemoaning poverty.
          I don't have enough to give a dowry for my grown-up
          daughter.
          So I can't contract her –
Meg: Oh, cheer up, Euclio.
          Marry she will – I'll help you. Tell me what you need.
Eu: [*aside*] My own cash he's promising. He hungers for my gold,
          holding bread in one hand and a big rock in the other.
          Never trust a rich man when he's civil to a pauper.
          When he shakes your hand he really wants to shake you
          down!
          He's just like an octopus – he's fastening his tentacles.
(E. Segal, *Plautus: Four Comedies*, World's Classics, 1996)

Molière's *The Miser* draws heavily on *The Pot of Gold*.

Another typical feature of Plautus, again drawn from Greek new comedy, is the tendency for humble characters to engage in moralising. Here, from *Rudens* (*The Rope*), a fisherman reflects:

Poor folks have a hard life of it every way, especially if they haven't any regular business and never learnt a trade. Whatever they have, that has simply got to do for 'em. As for us, you can just about tell what plutocrats we are from one look at our get-up. These hooks and rods here – that's how we subsist and flourish. Day in and day out, we foot it over from the city to the sea here to do some foraging: that's our exercise, our physical culture and wrestling. The parties we get a hold on are sea-urchins and limpets and oysters and shellfish and snails and sea-nettles and mussels and fluted scallops.

(Paul Nixon, *Plautus Vol IV*, Loeb Classical Library no. 260, Harvard-Heinemann, 1932)

Where Plautus breaks from Menandrian moralising and character-drawing is in the exuberance of his larger-than-life slave heroes and the outrageousness of their schemes. This can hardly have been true to life in Rome, where a slave's life was generally pretty grim. But this is holiday entertainment – and set in the Greek world anyway. Who knew what went on among those Greeks?

Here from *Bacchides*, Chrysalus ('Goldie') has brilliantly duped the father Nicobulus ('Victorious in counsel', ironically) out of 400 gold coins so that his son can buy the woman of his dreams. (Chrysalus has said he would do this, and likened himself to the Greek army taking Troy by the wooden horse trick. This explains his cry of triumph at the end.) So completely has Chrysalus deceived Nicobulus that Nicobulus even *orders* Chrysalus to take the gold! Chrysalus naturally pretends to decline:

N: Take this gold, Chrysalus. Go on, take it to my son.
C: Oh no, I absolutely won't take it! You go and find someone else to do it. I don't want this to be entrusted to me!
N: Take it! Don't annoy me.
C: Oh no, I absolutely won't have it.
N: Please.
C: I said that's that. And that's that.
N: Stop stalling.
C: I said I don't want the gold entrusted to me! Well, at least get somebody to keep guard on me.
N: Aaargh! You're getting me angry again.
C: Give it here, then, if you have to.
N: Now, see to this. I'll be back shortly.

C: I'll see to it [*pauses till N. is off-stage*] – see to it that you're the most wretched old fool alive! This is the way to finish: end with a flourish. How nicely things are going! What a Roman triumph! What a load of spoils! To make it official [*as if reading from a public decree*]: The public safety having been established, the town having been captured through guile, I lead our army un-harmed and whole back home. But don't be surprised if I don't celebrate a triumph now. They're far too common these days, spectators. My troops will have all the wine and honey they need. Now to carry this booty straight to the quartermaster! [*Enters the brothel.*]

(Slavitt and Bovie (eds), *Plautus: The Comedies. Vol II*, Johns Hopkins, 1995)

Observe how Chrysalus 'breaks the dramatic illusion' by referring directly to the spectators. Observe also how he 'romanises' the situation for the Roman audience by referring to the Roman practice of a triumph, and making a Roman-style decree.

Incidentally, Lord Byron's famous universal sob 'whom the gods love *die* young' is taken from Plautus *Bacchides*, where it is 'whom the gods love *dies* young' and is an insult directed by Chrysalus at Nicobulus – if the gods had loved him, he would not have lived so long and turned into such a 'rotten mushroom'. By a stroke of luck we have a papyrus fragment of the original Menander play on which *Bacchides* is based (*Dis exapaton* – 'the two-time trickster') and it contains these lines in Greek. Plautus, unlike Byron, translated them correctly.

Above all, perhaps, Plautus' language is more extreme, more violent, more full of puns, striking imagery and alliteration than Menander's. Plautus, clearly, knew his audience. Here, from *Pseudolus* again, the slave Pseudolus and his young master Calidorus publicly abuse the wonderfully shameless pimp Ballio. Ballio, naturally, owns the young girl that Calidorus is in love with, and Calidorus is pleading with him to give him a little more time to find the cash. Ballio, one of Plautus' finest creations, plays Calidorus along and then informs him he's sold the girl already:

Calidorus: Answer me! You most wicked man that ever walked the earth! Didn't you solemnly swear you wouldn't sell her to anyone but me?

Ballio: Exactly.

C: Indeed. And in legally binding terms.

B: That's right. Bound and gagged.

C: Well then, you've perjured yourself, you scoundrel!

B: But I've put money in my purse! And I, the scoundrel pimp, have got plenty in my pocket, while you the pious paragon, for all your pedigree, haven't got a penny pot to pee in!

C: Pseudolus, go stand over there and bombard him with insults.

Pseudolus: Delighted. Why, I wouldn't run faster for my freedom.

C: Crush him with curses!

P: I'll tear you to tatters with torment from my tongue! Wicked thing!

B: I like the ring!

C: Scoundrel!

B: It's true.

P: Hangdog!

B: Like you.

C: Tomb-robber!

B: I dare say.

P: Breaker of oaths!

C: Gallows bird!

B: The very word!

P: Scurvy slave!

B: Of course!

C: Unholy knave!

B: Endorsed!

P: Corrupter of youth!

B: Nicely expressed!

C: Perjurer!

B: I'm impressed!

P: Patricide!

B: I've nothing to hide.

C: Villain most vile!

B: I like your style!

P: Crock full of ca-ca!

B: La de bloody da da!

C: Filthy pimp!

B: Rather limp!
P: Slime!
B: Sublime!
C: Keeper of whores!
B: What a sweet chorus!
P: Utterly worthless!
B: At your service!
C: You abused your own mother and father!
B: Oh, I murdered them as well, to keep from feeding them. Nothing wrong in that, surely?
P: We're wasting our words, like water in a sieve.
B: Is there anything you wish to add?
C: Can nothing shame you?
B: I'd be ashamed to be like you. A lover, flat broke like an empty nut. Nevertheless, despite all the abuse you've heaped on me, I can promise you this: unless the soldier [*to whom Ballio has sold the girl*] comes up with the five *minae* that's due today on our 'lay-away' plan, I shall unhesitatingly fulfil my duty.
C: Which is?
B: Bring me the money yourself, my boy, and I shall dishonour my agreement with him. That's my pimpish duty. Now I'd just love to chat some more with you, but 'tempus fugit'! Now, no mistake: no money from you, no mercy from me. That's my position, so think it over, and act accordingly.
(Slavitt and Bovie (eds), *Plautus: The Comedies. Vol IV*)

This is wonderful knockabout stuff, verbal fireworks typical of Plautus at his best, and deeply influential on comedy down the ages.

The translations

Segal's translations are accurate and actable. Watling's too read well (nine plays in two volumes for Penguin). Slavitt and Bovie cover all Plautus in four very lively volumes, using a range of different translators. Nixon's Loeb (five volumes), with Latin, has lasted very well indeed.

13

Lucretius

Lucretius (*c*. 94-51 BC) is a poet with a mission: to lay, once and for all, the ghost of death. In this, he seems to be following an almost Christian agenda:

> For we, like children frightened of the dark,
> Are sometimes frightened in the light – of things
> No more to be feared than fears that in the dark
> Distress a child, thinking they may come true.
> Therefore this terror and darkness of the mind
> Not by the sun's rays, not the bright shafts of day,
> Must be dispersed, as is most necessary,
> But by the face of nature and her laws.
> (Sir Ronald Melville, *Lucretius: On the Nature of the Universe*,
> World's Classics, 1998)

But Lucretius' approach is the precise opposite of the Christian. In his wholly original six-book poem expounding a complete theory of the universe, he proves not that we triumph over death but that there is nothing after death. Our soul is mortal. It dies with us. Indeed, even religion itself is evil.

It is with this last proposition that Lucretius begins his great work. He gives as his example of religion's wickedness king Agamemnon sacrificing his daughter Iphigeneia so that he could get the wind he required to blow the Greek fleet to Troy. Agamemnon lured Iphigeneia to join them under the pretence that she would be marrying Achilles:

> Poor girl, what good did it do her then, that she
> Was the first to give the king the name of 'father'?
> Up to the altar the men escorted her, trembling;
> Not so that when the solemn rites were finished

She might be cheered in the ringing wedding hymn,
But filthily, at the marrying age, unblemished
Victim, she fell by her father's slaughter-stroke
To shove his fleet off on a bon voyage!
Such wickedness Religion can incite!
(Anthony Esolen, *Lucretius: On the Nature of Things*, Johns
Hopkins, 1995)

That the gods exist, of course, goes without saying:

The gods appear now and their quiet abodes
Which no winds ever shake, nor any rain
Falls on them from dark clouds, nor ever snow
Congealed with bitter frost with its white fall
Mars them; but always ever-cloudless air
Enfolds and smiles on them with bounteous light.
There nature everything supplies, and there
Through all the length of ages nothing comes
To vex the tranquil tenor of their minds.
But in contrast nowhere at all appear
The halls of Acheron.
(Melville)

But they live apart, have no hell and therefore have no interest in us:

The Gods, by right of Nature, must possess
An Everlasting Age, of perfect Peace:
Far off, remov'd from us, and our Affairs:
Neither approached by Dangers, or by Cares:
Rich in themselves, to whom we cannot add:
Not pleas'd by Good Deeds; nor provok'd by Bad.
(Earl of Rochester, in A. Poole and J. Maule (eds), *The Oxford
Book of Classical Verse in Translation*, Oxford, 1995)

Consequently, there is nothing to fear in death. Indeed, fear of death is
a major cause of evil in the world:

Consider too the blind greed and lust for status that drive pathetic
men to overstep the bounds of right and may even turn them into

100

accomplices or instruments of crime, struggling night and day with unstinted effort to scale the pinnacles of wealth. These running sores of life are fed in no small measure by fear of death. For abject ignominy and irksome poverty seem far indeed from the joy and assurance of life. From such a fate men revolt in groundless terror and long to escape far, far away. So in their greed of gain they amass a fortune out of civil bloodshed, piling wealth on wealth, they heap carnage on carnage.
(R.E. Latham, rev. J. Godwin, *Lucretius: On the Nature of the Universe*, Penguin, 1994)

But what about the soul? Does it not survive after death? Lucretius certainly agrees that we have a soul but, contradicting any number of Christian 'proofs of the immortality of the soul', he delivers a series of proofs of its mortality. The soul, he argues, is simply atoms which, like the body, re-join the universal atom-pool at death. Here he suggests that the soul ages like the body:

> What's more, mind and body are born
> Together, and grow old and weak together.
> For as babies toddle about with bodies soft
> And tender, so their minds are wobbly too.
> But when the trunk grows ripe with strength of adulthood
> The mind is better endowed, the reason stronger.
> And at last, when the might of Age has crushed the body,
> And the limbs have fallen, strengthless, beaten down,
> Then the native talent hobbles, the tongue wanders ...
> (Esolen)

But, given the usual attitude of ancients to death and Hades, how did this astonishingly perverse view come about? Lucretius' beliefs about death are built on his understanding of how the universe works, and this derives from the atomic theories of his hero, the Greek philosopher Epicurus (341-270 BC).

Lucretius expounds Epicurus' view that we and the world consist of nothing but atoms; he moves on to the mortality of the soul (at death our body and soul simply dissolve into their constituent atoms); discusses how phenomena like the senses, thought, sex and love work; describes how the world began and human civilisation developed; and ends with the great geological and celestial phenomena (earthquakes, lightning etc) which most of all make men believe in divine intervention in the world.

But, as we have seen, Lucretius has an ulterior motive in all this. The way the world is constructed has implications for the way we should behave in it. So Lucretius brilliantly interweaves physical science and ethics throughout the poem, and ultimately, for all the 'science', the poem is about man's place in the world and his prospects of happiness. Thus, for example, he urges:

> If one should guide his life by true principles, man's greatest riches is to live on a little, with contented mind; for a little is never lacking.
> (W.H.D. Rouse, rev. by M.F. Smith, *Lucretius: On the Nature of Things*, Loeb Classical Library no. 181, Harvard, 1992)

One of the most brilliant features of the poem is the imagination Lucretius brings to what he admits is a difficult task – turning complex physical science into poetry. As he admits to his patron Memmius, he was not even certain that the Latin language was up to it:

> Nor do I fail to see how hard it is
> To bring to light in Latin verse the dark
> Discoveries of the Greeks, especially
> Because of the poverty of our native tongue,
> And the novelty of the subjects of my theme.
> But still your merit, and as I hope, the joy
> Of our sweet friendship, urge me to toil
> And lead me on to watch through nights serene
> In my long quests for words, for poetry,
> By which to shine clear light before your mind
> To let you see into the heart of hidden things.
> (Melville)

But Lucretius succeeds brilliantly. How? He likens what he is doing to a doctor who, needing to treat children with nasty medicine, first smears honey round the rim of the cup. This poetic 'honey' takes the form of the most superbly realised images. Here Lucretius is trying to show how atoms, falling through infinite space, collide together to form the worlds:

> Observe what happens when sunbeams are admitted into a building and shed light on shadowy places. You will see a multitude of tiny particles mingling in a multitude of ways in the empty space within the actual beam of light, as though contending in everlasting conflict, rushing into battle rank upon rank with never a moment's pause in a rapid sequence of unions and disunions. From this you may picture what it is for the atoms to be perpetually tossed about in the illimitable void.
> (Latham, rev. Godwin)

Here Lucretius explains how atoms, though in constant motion, appear to stand motionless in solid objects (unless, of course, the object moves of its own free will). This is because atoms are below the level of perception, and so their movements must be too. He goes on:

> For often on a hill, cropping the rich pasture, woolly sheep go creeping whither the herbage, all gemmed with fresh dew, tempts and invites each, and full-fed the lambs play and butt heads in fun; all of which things are seen by us blurred together in the distance, as a kind of whiteness at rest on a green hill.
> (Rouse, rev. Smith)

Here Lucretius uses a metaphor of childbirth by Caesarian section to underpin the ferocity with which a thunderbolt rips out of a cloud:

> At other times a violent squall of wind falls upon a cloud already pregnant with a full-grown thunderbolt. The wind rips open the cloud, and in that moment out drops that fiery whirlwind which is what we in our traditional language call a thunderbolt.
> (Latham, rev. Godwin)

Sunbeams, sheep, pregnancy – the fertility of Lucretius' imagination is astonishing, as he wrestles to make clear the physical working of the universe in language everyone can understand. So Lucretius' fears were groundless. His six-book poem expounding Epicurus' theory of the universe is the most brilliantly original masterpiece in the Latin language. But he would be appalled to see how, for all his efforts, in the twentieth century fear of death still looms as large as ever it did.

The translations

Both Esolen (who pays close attention to the imagery) and Melville opt to turn poetry into poetry, and go for a successful, loose blank verse. Both have introductions and full notes, as does Godwin's revision of Latham (prose), which also usefully marks the steps of the argument by italics in the text. Smith's revision of Rouse in the Loeb series (with facing page Latin) is very accurate.

14

Catullus

Everybody loves a lover, and they do not come more lover-ly than Gaius Valerius Catullus (*c*. 84-54 BC):

> Dear Lesbia, let us love and play,
> Not caring what Old Age can say;
> The Sun does set, again does rise,
> And with fresh Lustre gild the Skies.
> When once extinguisht is our Light,
> Wee're wrapt in everlasting Night.
> A thousand times my lips then kiss
> An hundred more renew the bliss;
> Another thousand add to these,
> An hundred more will not suffice,
> Another thousand will not do,
> Another hundred are too few.
> A thousand more these Joyes wee'll prove,
> Till wee're extravagant in Love,
> Till no malicious Spie can ghess
> To what a wonderful Excess
> My Lesbia and I did kiss.
> (John Chatwin, in A. Poole and J. Maule (eds), *The Oxford Book of Classical Verse in Translation*, Oxford, 1995)

Sweet! But if one objects that this is nothing new – it's the sort of thing you find in the love poetry of the Greek epigrams we looked at in Chapter 11 – it is pretty new in Latin poetry. Second, and far more important, it is clear that Catullus thinks about his relationship with Lesbia in terms other than the purely physical:

Lesbia for ever on me rails:
    To talk on me she never fails:
Yet, hang me, but for all her Art,
    I find that I have gain'd her heart:
My proof is thus: I plainly see
    The Case is just the same with me:
I curse her evr'y hour sincerely;
Yet, hang me, but I love her dearly.
(Jonathan Swift, in Poole and Maule)

This is not quite the way that the sex-obsessed Greek epigrammatists wrote about their feelings or their lovers. Nor do their poems deal in uncertainty in the way that Catullus' do:

Joy of my life! You tell me this –
That nothing can possibly break this love of ours for each other.
God let her mean what she says,
              From a candid heart,
That our two lives may be linked in their length
Day to day,
      Each to each,
In a bond of sacred fidelity.
(Peter Whigham, *Catullus*, Penguin, 1966)

Bonds? Sacred fidelity? No, bed will do fine for me, you can hear the Greeks saying, till the next one comes long. But Catullus is exploring and thinking about his feelings for Lesbia in quite a new way, and there is something of a desperation about his hopes here.

Lesbia (the pet name Catullus used for her) was probably in real life Clodia, wife of Metellus (consul in 60 BC). Catullus was one of a smart set of young poets on the make, well versed in Greek poetry (especially the epigrammatists), and seeing what they could do with this sort of poetry in Latin. They moved among arty, educated Romans in high society.

That Catullus should be having an affair with the wife of the consul may be thought foolish, and to boast about it in poetry even more foolish. But this was Rome of the first century BC, when adultery was on the increase and aristocratic woman, observing the developing, fashionable demi-monde of high-class courtesans in Rome, began to see

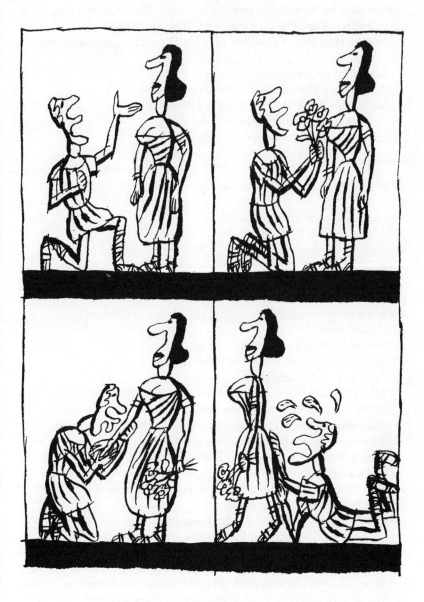

possibilities for themselves outside marriage. This was, perhaps, their form of liberation. The question was – how far to go?

Not far enough, for Catullus anyway. The affair came to an end:

> Ruined by its own devotion and the great
> Wrongs you have done it, Lesbia, to this state
> My heart's reduced now: that I'll wish you ill
> Though you become a paragon, and still
> Love you, whatever crime you perpetrate.
> (James Michie, *Catullus*, Wordsworth Classics, 1998)

This, famously, became condensed down to:

> I hate her – yet I love her too.
> > You ask how this can be.
> I only know that it is true
> > And bitter agony.
> (Janet Maclean Todd in Michael Grant (ed), *Latin Literature*, Penguin, 1978)

Here Catullus tries and fails to look ahead to a Lesbia-free future:

> You had better stop playing the fool, Catullus,
> And accept that what you see is lost, is lost.
> Once your days were shining
> When you used to go wherever the girl led you,
> She loved as none will ever be loved.
> Then those many pleasant things were done
> Which you wanted and the girl was willing to do;
> Certainly then your days were shining.
> She wants those things no more: you had better not want them,
> Nor ask for what will not be given, nor live in pain.
> Be patient, harden your mind.
> Goodbye, girl. Already Catullus is hardened.
> He does not seek you, and will not, since you are unwilling.
> But you will suffer when you are asked for nothing at night.
> It is the end. What life remains for you?
> Who now will come to you? Who will think you pretty?
> Whom will you now love? Whose will you say you are?
> Whom will you kiss? And whose lips will you bite?

But you, Catullus, accept fate and be firm.
(C.H. Sisson, *Collected Translations*, Carcanet, 1996)

Observe the structure of the poem – Catullus first moves from the present, to the past, and back to the present again. He then reaffirms his decision to accept fate. But then he thinks of Lesbia, in more and more intimate terms as the memories come flooding back, and has to pull himself up with a start at the end. He is trying to distance himself from the whole experience, and failing.

And of course, it turned nasty, as it always does. Here Catullus confides in his friend Caelius:

My Lesbia, Caelius, that same Lesbia
Whom once Catullus loved more than himself
And all his own, now in the alleyways
And at the street corners milks with a practised hand
The upright members of magnanimous Rome.
(Humphrey Clucas, in Poole and Maule)

But there is more to Catullus' poetry than Lesbia. The young poets in whose circle he moved experimented with subjects as varied as the Greek epigrams they knew so well, and Catullus tried his hand at some mini-epics too. Here he wittily pleads poverty:

You'll dine well, my Fabullus, at mine
One day soon if the Gods are kind to you,
If you will bring with you a dinner
Good and large plus a pretty girl
And wine and salt and all the laughs.
If, I repeat, you bring these with you,
Our charmer, you'll dine well; for your
Catullus' purse is full of cobwebs.
But in return you'll get love neat
Or something still more choice and fragrant;
For I'll provide the perfume given
My girl by Venuses and Cupids
And when you smell it you'll ask the Gods,
Fabullus, to make you one large nose.
(Guy Lee, *The Poems of Catullus*, World's Classics, 1990)

Here he gets personal with someone who stinks and suffers from gout:

> If anyone ever deserves such underarm goatodour
>   Or ever merited gout's terrible swellings,
> It's that rival of yours, who's sharing not only your mistress
>   But – quite miraculously – your diseases also!
> Whenever he fucks her, both of them suffer your vengeance:
>   She gets your goat and he's the one your gout gets.
> (Charles Martin, *The Poems of Catullus*, Johns Hopkins, 1979)

Here he movingly consoles Calvus on the loss of his wife:

> Calvus, if sorrow for the dead, the pain
>   That brings past love achingly back again
> And makes us mourn missed friendship, ever gave
>   Pleasure or solace to the speechless grave,
> Your love must give Quintilia, your dead wife,
>   Joy to outweigh loss of so young life.
> (Michie)

Catullus is a highly innovative poet of the Latin language. As we have seen with other Latin poets, he is looking back to the Greek but creating something fresh and original and wholly Roman out of it. He is beginning to push Latin poetry into corners it has not explored before, sexual and personal, and to extend its range over new styles and subject-matters. Later poets will enthusiastically pick up Catullus' torch.

The translations

Poole and Maule have a good selection of witty ancient and modern efforts. Whigham's poems are either fireworks or duds. Sisson opts for a plain, easy style. Lee, a fine scholar, combines accuracy with felicity (with facing-page Latin and good notes). Those who like rhyme may prefer Michie's very clever efforts. Martin is sound and intelligent. Michael Grant's anthology covers Latin prose and poetry from Plautus to St Augustine.

15

Virgil

Why does a culture suddenly start sprouting seriously high-class poets? Lucretius and Catullus should have been quite enough for first-century BC Rome, but they kept on coming. Enter Publius Vergilius Maro (70-19 BC), Virgil, the most famous of them all.

Virgil's world was one of political turmoil and bloodshed. Republican Rome with its traditional, ordered government of Senate and annually appointed consuls was being ripped apart by power-hungry dynasts like Pompey and Caesar who, representing no one but themselves, used their personal military following to destroy the republic and impose their own will upon it. In 48 BC Caesar claimed the 'crown' (Pompey was left a headless corpse on an Egyptian beach), only to be assassinated in 44 BC. More civil war, more blood. In 31 BC Octavian, Caesar's adopted son and heir, the future emperor Augustus, emerged victorious against Marc Antony and Cleopatra. What *now*? The same old pattern? More blood?

Virgil cut his poetic teeth on what to us is a most unlikely poetic genre – pastoral, invented by Theocritus, a Greek poet living in Sicily in the third century BC. In Virgil's *Eclogues*, assorted shepherds and goatherds tootle away to each other on their pipes, singing of their lives and loves (today's *Eclogues* would depict office-workers exchanging e-mails). For Virgil, the country life was somehow hallowed, sacred. The good old Roman was a farmer, close to the soil and therefore close to the essential nature and meaning of things. Virgil was 'green' through and through. But the years of civil war had thrown this life into turmoil, and in his *Eclogues* (published *c*. 38 BC) Virgil starts gently to explore the possibilities of comparing country life with political life, to see what light the one might cast on the other – or whether they can co-exist at all. Here Virgil famously sees a golden age returning with the birth of a child, and earth effortlessly pouring out its bounty, unworked:

111

The great succession of centuries is born afresh.
Now too returns the Virgin [*goddess of justice*]; Saturn's rule
    returns [*he ruled during the last golden age*];
A new begetting now descends from heaven's height.
O chaste Lucina [*goddess of childbirth*], look with blessing on the boy
Whose birth will end the iron race at last and raise
A golden through the world ...
(Guy Lee, *Virgil: The Eclogues*, Penguin, 1984)

The child is probably the hoped-for son of Marc Antony through marriage to Octavian/Augustus' sister Octavia (40 BC) – but Antony's affair with Cleopatra soon wrecked that hope. Christians, inevitably, interpreted this *Eclogue* as foreshadowing the birth of Jesus.

This poem was Virgil's passport into the literary circle of the fabulously wealthy Maecenas, Rome's greatest patron of the arts, and friend and agent of Octavian/Augustus – no modern Minister of Culture has ever wielded such influence. Virgil's next work, *Georgics* (*c.* 29 BC), takes much further the theme of country and political life. In four books on the work of the farmer (Book 1 crops; Book 2 trees and shrubs; Book 3 livestock; Book 4 bees), Virgil combines agricultural instruction with reflection on the nature of the world and man's place in it. But since the poem is addressed to the city sophisticate Maecenas, one should not take its educational function too literally (one cannot imagine a Minister for Culture rushing out to his country estates to sow and plough naked just because Virgil recommended it). This is a call for a return to ancient values in the shape of praise of the virtues of country life. Here Virgil reflects on what has gone wrong in Rome:

For right and wrong change places; everywhere
So many wars, so many shapes of crime
Confront us; no due honour attends the plough,
The fields, bereft of tillers, are all unkempt.
And in the forge the curving pruning-hook
Is made a straight hard sword. Euphrates here [*a river in the east,
    modern Iraq*],
There Germany is in arms, and neighbour cities
Break covenants and fight; throughout the world
Impious War is raging. As on a racecourse,
The barriers down, out pour the chariots,

Gathering speed from lap to lap, and a driver
Tugging in vain at the reins is swept along
By his horses and heedless uncontrollable car.
(L.P. Wilkinson, *Virgil: The Georgics*, Penguin, 1982)

The *Georgics* is a magnificent poem. It has, perhaps unfairly, been outshone by the final masterpiece that Virgil bequeathed to us in response to this political turmoil. Begun in the early 20s BC as Augustus began to impose himself and bring order to Rome again, Virgil's *Aeneid* is an epic – the story of the founding of the Roman race. The poem begins:

Arms, and the Man I sing, who forc'd by Fate,
And haughty Juno's unrelenting Hate;
Expell'd and exil'd, left the Trojan Shoar:
Long Labours, both by Land and Sea he bore;
…
From whence the Race of Alban Fathers come,
And the long glories of Majestick Rome.
(F.M. Keener (ed), *Virgil's Aeneid translated by John Dryden*, Penguin, 1997)

The 'man' is Aeneas, who fled the burning city of Troy as it was being sacked by Greeks, and with a band of Trojans set out on the high seas for Italy. The pro-Greek goddess Juno hated them and harried them all the way. But their mission was divinely ordained. The Trojan settlers finally landed in Italy and after fighting off local opposition settled in Alba Longa. This is the story the *Aeneid* tells. It was the Trojans' descendant Romulus, some three hundred years later (by myth-histori-cal reckoning), who founded Rome in 753 BC.

As we have already seen, Roman poets drew their inspiration from the Greeks, and Virgil here has one eye firmly on Homer. 'Arms' and 'Juno's unrelenting Hate' remind us of the battles of the *Iliad* and Achilles' wrath; the 'Man' who bore 'Long Labours' by land and sea reminds us of Odysseus' travels to reach his home in the *Odyssey*. But Aeneas trumps both Achilles (doomed to die) and Odysseus (who merely returned home): his story, powerfully and patriotically, will reach its fated end in 'the long glories of Majestick Rome'. The gods too have their parts to play. As Homer before him, Virgil manipulates them

113

at will for his own narrative purposes, without much care for theological consistency, creating out of them a squabbling family ruled by a benign but determined father, Jupiter, who ensures that nothing ultimately stands in the way of his plans for Aeneas.

The structure of the *Aeneid* too reflects the *Odyssey-Iliad* connection. In the first six 'Odyssean' books, we are told how Aeneas leaves Troy and after various adventures on the seas and a visit to the underworld (just like Odysseus) arrives in Italy; in the last six 'Iliadic' books, Aeneas allies himself with the local king Latinus and fights off the opposition to his arrival, led by Turnus. The *Aeneid* ends with Aeneas killing Turnus in single combat (cf. Achilles and Hector in the *Iliad*, p. 11).

At one level the *Aeneid* is a highly political poem. It was composed as Augustus was pulling Rome to its feet after the horrors of the civil war years. Like all Romans, Virgil had reason to be profoundly grateful to Augustus and constantly makes connections between Aeneas, who founded Rome, and Augustus, who, after the civil wars, is *re*founding it. As in *Eclogues* and *Georgics*, Virgil is setting two worlds side by side – in this case, ancient epic and modern politics – to see how they respond to each other. In the process, he is constructing an image of Augustus that will ring down the generations. Indeed, one of the main reasons why we regard Augustus as a great man is precisely because great poets celebrated him. Maecenas had chosen wisely.

Here, Aeneas is in the underworld consulting his dead father, Anchises. Anchises encourages him in his mission by pointing out the future heroes of Rome and showing him the glories that are to come. He ends by stating that other peoples (he means Greeks) will be better at the arts, oratory and sciences:

'But you, Roman, remember, you are to rule
The nations of the world: your arts will be
To bring the ways of peace, be merciful
To the defeated and smash the proud completely.'
(C.H. Sisson, *Virgil: The Aeneid*, Carcanet, 1986)

Virgil constantly makes his characters 'foresee' the glories of Augustan Rome to come, and these words are pure Augustanism. Then Aeneas sees a young man, Marcellus, with a shadow dark as night around his head. Anchises explains:

15. Virgil

'My son, do not probe into the sorrows of your kin.
Fate shall allow the earth one glimpse of this young man –
One glimpse, no more. Too puissant had been Rome's stock, ye gods,
In your sight, had such gifts been granted it to keep.
What lamentations of men shall the Campus Martius echo
To Mars' great city [*Rome*]! O Tiber, what obsequies you shall see
One day as you glide past the new-built Mausoleum ...
... Give me armfuls of lilies
That I may scatter their shining blooms and shower these gifts
At least upon the dear soul, all to no purpose though
Such kindness be.'
(C. Day-Lewis, *The Aeneid of Virgil*, World's Classics, 1995)

This young Marcellus whom Anchises 'foresees' was the son of Augustus' sister Octavia. Augustus adopted him as his son in 25 BC, but he died aged 19 in 23 BC. Virgil probably witnessed the funeral and writes it into this passage. We are told that, when Virgil finished reading this section aloud to Augustus and Octavia, she swooned.

While the *Aeneid* constantly looks to Augustan Rome, however, it is not propaganda (how many Romans read poetry anyway?). These are flesh and blood heroes and for Aeneas in particular, called *pius* ('dutiful') by Virgil a bit too often for modern taste, things are by no means so easy. In Book 4, Aeneas, having arrived in Carthage in North Africa, begins an affair with the local queen, Dido. This will not do. Jupiter sends the messenger god Mercury to remind him of his mission. Aeneas, stunned, struck dumb, prepares to leave, but Dido ('for who can deceive a lover?') senses what is happening and confronts him:

'... for you
my honour is gone and that good name that once
was mine, my only claim to reach the stars.
My guest, to whom do you consign this dying
Woman? I must say "guest": this name is all
I have of one whom once I called my husband.
... Had I at least before you left conceived
a son in me; if there were but a tiny
Aeneas playing by me in the hall,
whose face, in spite of everything, might yet
remind me of you, then indeed I should

not seem so totally abandoned, beaten.'
(A. Mandelbaum, *The Aeneid of Virgil*, California, 1981)

Aeneas pleads 'It is not my own free will that leads to Italy' and deadlock is reached:

> For lamentation cannot move Aeneas;
> His graciousness towards any plea is gone.
> Fate is opposed, the god makes deaf the hero's
> Kind ears. As when, along the Alps, north winds
> Will strain against each other to root out
> With blasts – now on this side, now that – a stout
> Oak tree whose wood is full of years; the roar
> Is shattering, the trunk is shaken, and
> High branches scatter on the ground; but it
> Still grips the rocks; as steeply as it thrusts
> Its crown into the upper air, so deep
> The roots it reaches down to Tartarus:
> No less than this, the hero: he is battered
> On this side and on that by assiduous words;
> He feels care in his mighty chest, and yet
> His mind cannot be moved: the tears fall, useless.
> (Mandelbaum)

Note the magnificent simile, inserted at a moment of high emotion (as often in Homer too) and carefully connected point by point to the narrative, as usual in Virgil (Aeneas is battered; this side and that; by words; he feels care; but is not moved; and tears fall. So the tree is battered; this side and that; by winds; the trunk is shaken; but it still grips the rocks; and branches fall).

Aeneas departs. Dido commits suicide on a pyre, claiming that she will not die unavenged. Here Virgil signals another piece of history, the origins of the Punic wars, fought between Carthage (most famously under Hannibal) and Rome in the third century BC. But if Aeneas = Augustus, this episode is not a very complimentary one. The emperor will not be pleased to be associated with beach-side affairs with a wild-eyed foreign floozie, let alone a Carthaginian one, let alone one that resulted in the devastating Punic wars. One-dimensional the *Aeneid*

116

is not. Great scholars nod sagely and call it 'problematic' – as if that solves anything.

What one can say is that Virgil does not attempt to suppress the price that had to be paid for founding Rome. Dido (and so the Punic wars) is one such price. Aeneas pays a personal price too. When he makes an alliance in Italy with a local king Evander, he promises to protect his son Pallas in battle. But Pallas is killed and when Aeneas sees the body, he cries:

> 'This is not what I promised Evander for his son ... even now, deluded by vain hopes, he may be making vows and heaping altars with offerings, while we bring him with tears and useless honours a young warrior who owes no more debts to any heavenly power. With what eyes will you look at the dead body of your son? Is this how we return from war? Are these the triumphs expected of us? Is this my great pledge?'
> (D.A. West, *Virgil: The Aeneid*, Penguin, 1990)

And as Pallas is buried, Aeneas groans:

> 'The same grim destiny of war calls us away from here to weep other tears. For ever hail, great Pallas, and farewell for ever.'
> (West)

Then again, the pity of war is superbly caught in the death of Priam, the old king of Troy, who, seeing his son killed and despite the pleas from his wife, 'buckled his armour long unused on shoulders trembling with age' to be mercilessly cut down by Achilles' degenerate son Neoptolemus:

> 'Now, die.' As he spoke the word, he was dragging Priam to the very altar, his body trembling as it slithered through pools of his son's blood. Winding Priam's hair in his left hand, in his right he raised the sword with a flash of light and buried it to the hilt in Priam's side.
> So ended the destiny of Priam. This was the death that fell to his lot. He who once had been the proud ruler over so many lands and peoples of Asia died with Troy ablaze before his eyes and the

citadel of Pergamum in ruins. His mighty trunk lay upon the shore, the head hacked from the shoulders, a corpse without a name. (West)

Does that headless corpse, oddly transported to the shore though Priam was killed at the altar in Troy, remind us of Pompey, slaughtered on an Egyptian beach?

'Something greater than the *Iliad* is being born' said the Roman poet Propertius, Virgil's contemporary, of the *Aeneid*. Not quite. But nearly.

The translations

Lee's *Eclogues* (with facing-page Latin) and Wilkinson's *Georgics* are the work of fine scholars (both with excellent introductions and notes), the translations elegant and accurate. For the *Aeneid*, Dryden's translation, celebrating its 300th birthday in 1997, is a classic in its own right (also available in Wordsworth Classics, edited by James Morwood). Of the other poetic versions, Sisson is consistently straightforward, but rarely rises to great heights; Day-Lewis is somewhat uneven; Mandelbaum strikes me as the most successful. West's prose translation is clear, accurate and forceful. *Virgil in English* (ed. K.W. Gransden, Penguin, 1996) gives a taste of translations from Chaucer to Seamus Heaney.

16

Ovid

Every culture has its joker. In the exuberantly talented world of Augustan Rome, this honour falls to Publius Ovidius Naso (43 BC-AD 17), Ovid. Asked which line of his poetry he would consign to the flames, he said (from the Minotaur story), 'A half-bull man, a half-man bull.' And which line would he keep? 'A half-bull ...' Very Oscar Wilde, very Ovid.

Here is part of his *Art of Love*, a brilliant tongue-in-cheek manual on how to woo, win and keep a lover, with constant reference to myths giving examples how, and how not, to do it:

> I'll give you specific advice, now, on just what limits
>   You should set to your drinking. Keep mind and feet
> Steady. Above all, avoid drunken quarrels, don't get
>   Into a fight too fast.
> His stupid swilling killed off Eurytion the Centaur:
> Wine over dinner was meant rather to promote
> Fun and games ...
> But when the tables are cleared, and the guests departing,
>   And in the confusion you perceive your chance
> To make contact, then join the crowd, discreetly approach her
>   On the way out, let you finger brush against
> Her side, touch her foot with yours. Now's the time for chatting
>   Her up, no clodhopping bashfulness – the bold
> Are favoured by Chance and Venus. Don't think that your eloquence
>   Must conform to poetic canons. Just pitch in
> And you'll find yourself fluent enough. You must play the lover,
>   Ape heartache with words, use every subtle device
> To compel her belief. It's not hard – what woman doesn't believe she's
>   A natural object for love, or, however plain,
> Isn't thrilled by her own appearance?
> (Peter Green, *Ovid: The Erotic Poems*, 1982, Penguin)

But who but Ovid, having solemnly composed this witty treatise on how to get into a love-affair, should promptly publish *Remedies for Love*, with instructions on how to get out of it again?

All this fun and games, however, got Ovid into trouble with the strait-laced emperor Augustus. We do not know precisely what happened, but in AD 8 Augustus suddenly exiled him to Tomis on the Black Sea (Constanta, in Romania). Here he wrote poetic letters to Augustus and his successor Tiberius pleading for his return:

> Ah, why did I ever study? Why did my parents
>   give me an education? Why did I learn
> so much as ABC? It was my *Art* [*of Love*]'s wantonness turned you
>   against me, because you were convinced
> it encouraged illicit sex. But no brides have become intriguers
>   through me: no one can teach what he does not know.
> Yes, I've written frivolous verses, erotic poems – but never
>   has a breath of scandal touched my name. There's no
> husband, even among the lower classes, who questions
>   his paternity through any fault of mine!
> My morals, believe me, are quite distinct from my verses –
>   a respectable life-style, a flirtatious Muse –
> and the larger part of my writings is mendacious, fictive,
>   assumes the licence its author denies himself.
> (Peter Green, *Ovid: The Poems of Exile*, Penguin, 1994)

To no avail. Ovid died in exile in AD 17.

Fortunately for the world, Ovid's great masterpiece, *Metamorphoses* ('Transformations'), had already been completed. This gloriously lunatic work in fifteen books is a vast mock epic. The basic *mise-en-scène* is Olympus, where the gods chat among themselves. With fiendish narrative ingenuity (involving changes of scene and narrator, usually through 'Chinese box' stories within stories) Ovid uses this setting to string together almost every myth known to man involving a change of shape. This huge canvas gives full scope to his formidably inventive imagination, revealing in their full glory his wit, powers of observation and description, and sympathetic understanding of human character, aspirations and suffering.

Jupiter has turned his lover Io into a cow to avoid the wrath of his suspicious wife Juno. What if one were turned into a cow without quite realising it, thinks Ovid (he is the poet of 'what if?'), especially when you are left to graze in the fields of your father Inachus? And how do you tell him of your plight?

> She grazed on the leaves of trees and on the bitter grass,
> And instead of a bed, unhappy one, she lay on not always
> Grassy earth and drank from muddy rivers.
> When she wanted to stretch her arms out to Argus [*her guard*]
> In supplication, she had no arms to stretch out to Argus.
> And when she tried to complain, her mouth let forth a mooing,
> And she was afraid of the sound and terrified by her own voice.
> She came to the banks, where she often used to play,
> To Inachus' banks, and when she saw her new horns
> In the water, she was afraid and fled from herself in consternation.
> The Naiads [*water-nymphs*] did not know, Inachus himself did not
>   know
> Who she was. But she followed her father and she followed her sisters
> And let herself be petted and offered herself to be admired ...
>   ... if only speech had come,
> she would have begged for help and told her name and her misfortune.
> Instead of speech, it was lettering which her foot traced in the dust
> That brought about the sad disclosure of her transformation.
> (D.E. Hill, *Ovid: Metamorphoses I-IV*, Aris and Phillips, 1985)

This is one long GCSE-style empathy exercise. First, thinks Ovid, she has to eat. What will she think about what she finds herself knocking back? Euurgh! Leaves! Bitter grass! Then she must drink (muddy rivers!) and sleep (not always grassy ground!). No arms to supplicate with ... mooing in place of a voice ... then she sees herself in the water. Horns! Not a fashion statement. So how can she communicate? Think, Ovid, think – ah, got it: by writing with her hoof in the dust. This is all beautifully observed and very funny and in its way rather moving.

Here the horrible, hairy, rustic one-eyed Cyclops Polyphemus is trying to woo the sea-nymph Galatea, who is in fact in love with Acis. But how does such a monster make a case? Galatea tells us part of what he sang to her:

> ... See how large I am!
> No bigger body Jove himself could boast

Up in the sky – you always talk of Jove
Or someone reigning there. My ample hair
O'erhangs my grave stern face and like a grove
Darkens my shoulders; and you must not think
Me ugly, that my body is so thick
With prickly bristles. Trees without their leaves are ugly …
Upon my brow I have one single eye,
But it is huge, like some vast shield. What then?
Does not the mighty sun see from the sky
All things on earth? Yet the sun's orb is one.'
(A.D. Melville, *Ovid's Metamorphoses*, World's Classics, 1986)

Poor Cyclops! Quite sweet really. No wonder maritime sophisticates like Galatea had no time for him.

Here the handsome young Narcissus, who has spurned all advances, has caught a glimpse of his own face in the water, and fallen for – himself:

He lay, like a fallen garden statue,
Gaze fixed on his image in the water,
Comparing it to Bacchus or Apollo,
Falling deeper and deeper in love
With what so many had loved so hopelessly.
Not recognising himself
He wanted only himself.
He had chosen
From all the faces he had ever seen
Only his own. He was himself
The torturer who now began to torture.
He plunged his arms deep to embrace
One who vanished in agitated water.
Again and again he kissed
The lips that seemed to be rising to kiss his
But dissolved as he touched them,
Into a soft splash and a shiver of ripples.
(Ted Hughes, *Tales from Ovid*, Faber and Faber, 1997)

Ovid adores these sorts of human paradoxes (which for some reason get

modern scholars frothing with excitement) and exploits them to the full.

Finally, Baucis and Philemon, a poor but loving old couple who, unknowing, entertained Jupiter and Mercury in disguise. The whole story is lovingly observed, as the poverty-struck, honest couple do their best not to let the side down. I underline some of the deliciously sympathetic touches:

> When the heaven-dwellers reached this <u>humble</u> home and, <u>stooping</u> down, entered its <u>low</u> doorway, the old man set chairs for them, and invited them to rest their weary limbs; Baucis bustled up <u>anxiously</u> to throw a <u>rough piece of cloth</u> over the chairs, and stirred up the warm ashes on the hearth, fanning the remains of <u>yesterday's</u> fire, feeding it with <u>leaves and chips of dried bark</u>, and blowing on it till it burst into flames. Then the old woman took down finely split sticks and dried twigs which were <u>hanging from the roof</u>, broke them into small pieces, and pushed them under her <u>little</u> pot. Her husband brought in some <u>vegetables</u> from his <u>carefully watered</u> garden, and these she stripped of their outer leaves. Philemon took a two-pronged fork and lifted down a side of smoked bacon that was hanging from the <u>blackened</u> rafters; then he cut off a <u>small</u> piece of their <u>long-cherished</u> meat, and boiled it till it was tender in the bubbling water. Meanwhile the old couple chattered on, to pass the time and <u>keep their guests from noticing the delay</u>.
> (M. Innes, *Ovid: Metamorphoses*, Penguin, 1955)

The couple are, of course, rewarded, and given their last wish – to die together. When that time comes, they are turned into trees, with cries of 'Goodbye, my dear one' simultaneously on their lips.

Ovid was a joker – a genius of a joker. But go to any art gallery, and it is Ovid's account of a myth that will have caught the artist's eye. Read sixteenth- and seventeenth-century poetry, and Ovid will be there somewhere.

The translations

Melville's blank verse is always fluent and easy. Green's *The Erotic Poems* catches the wit and cynicism of Ovid very well; his *Poems of Exile* are (rightly) more solemn in tone (both with very full, scholarly notes). Hill's edition (with facing-page Latin and commentary on the English) is accurate and helpful. Ted Hughes' translation-cum-paraphrase is pure class. Innes' elegant, clear prose version has lasted well. Christopher Martin's *Ovid in English* (Penguin, 1998) offers versions from Chaucer to Ted Hughes and Seamus Heaney, including lengthy extracts from perhaps Ovid's greatest translator, Arthur Golding (1536-1606), whose *Metamorphoses* powerfully influenced Shakespeare.

17

Seneca

Roman writers tended to have close political links. Virgil, for example, was one of a number of poets brought under the first emperor Augustus' wing by his minister for culture Maecenas; and Ovid's connections in high places led, eventually, to his exile.

Lucius Annaeus Seneca (the younger, *c*. AD 1-65) is in this respect the most interesting Roman writer of all. Not only was he prolific and successful in both Latin prose and verse (and a multi-millionaire) but he also played a critical role in guiding Nero (emperor AD 54-68) through his early years on the throne. So what does one make of this chorus from one of Seneca's nine surviving tragedies, *Thyestes*?

> Let others scale dominion's slippery peak;
> Peace and obscurity are all I seek.
> Enough for me to live alone, and please
> Myself with idleness and leisured ease.
> A man whose name his neighbours would not know,
> I'd watch my stream of life serenely flow
> Through quiet years of darkness, until the day
> When an old man, a commoner, passed away.
> Death's terrors are for him who, too well known,
> Will die a stranger to himself alone.
> (E.F. Watling, *Four Tragedies and Octavia*, Penguin, 1966)

The answer is – one cannot make much. Teasing though it is to try to draw conclusions from the fact that this was written by a man with the wealth and power of Seneca, we cannot fillet out portions of plays and claim they represent the author's 'real' feelings. This is a play. The chorus is well suited to a work in which the crazed king Atreus, greedy for revenge against his brother Thyestes, kebabs Thyestes' sons and serves them up to him at a banquet.

17. Seneca

What is interesting is how such quiet reflection sits side by side with such appalling violence in Seneca's tragedies. Quentin Tarantino had nothing on Seneca.

Here a messenger describes how Oedipus, having discovered that he has killed his father and married his mother, blinded himself. You are advised to have a bowl handy:

> suddenly he began to weep   everything that had been torment
> suddenly it was sobbing   it shook his whole body and he shouted
>   is weeping all I can give can't my eyes give any more   let them
> go with their tears   let them go   eyeballs too   everything out
>   is this enough for you you frozen gods of marriage   is it
> sufficient   are my eyes enough
>
> he was raging as he spoke   his face throbbed dark red   his
> eyeballs seemed to be jumping in their sockets   forced out from
> the skull   his face was no longer the face of Oedipus   contorted
> like a rabid dog   he had begun to scream   a bellowing animal
>   anger   agony tearing his throat
>
> his fingers had stabbed deep into his sockets   he hooked them
> gripping his eyeballs   and he tugged twisting and dragging with
> all his strength   till they gave way   and he flung them from him
>   his fingers dug back into his sockets he could not stop he was
> gibbering and moaning insane with his fury against himself
> gouging   scrabbling with his nails
> in those huge holes in his face
> the terrors of the light are finished for Oedipus
> he lifted his face   with its raw horrible gaps
> he tested the darkness
> there were rags of flesh strings and nerve ends
> still trailing over his cheeks   he fumbled for them
> snapping them off   every last shred
> then he let out a roar   half-screamed
> you gods
> now will you stop torturing my country
> I've found the murderer   and look   I've punished him
> I've forced him to pay the debt
> and his marriage   I've found the darkness for it

as he was screaming his face seemed to blacken suddenly
the blood vessels had burst inside his torn eyepits
the blood came spewing out over his face and beard
in a moment he was drenched
(Ted Hughes, *Seneca's Oedipus*, Faber and Faber, 1969)

Not much classical restraint there. One can imagine someone like Nero reading it and taking enthusiastic notes. But it is obvious why Seneca had such appeal to renaissance tragedians, including Shakespeare, both for his powerful declamatory style and visual imagination (remember Gloucester and his eyeballs in *King Lear*).

Even more interesting are Seneca's 124 letters and 12 treatises. These are written from a primarily Stoic point of view and are full of advice about the purpose of existence – personally, to search for wisdom (self-sufficiency, inner calm, immunity to the buffetings of chance, condemnation of power, wealth and emotionalism) and publicly, to serve the state and, indeed, the wider world (it was the Stoics who articulated the idea of the world-citizen). Here Seneca urges humane treatment of slaves:

'He's a slave.' But he may have the spirit of a free man. 'He's a slave.' But is that really to count against him? Show me a man who isn't a slave; one is a slave to sex, another to money, another to ambition; all are slaves to hope and fear. I could show you a man who has been Consul who is a slave to his 'little old woman', a millionaire who is the slave of a girl in domestic service. I could show you some highly aristocratic young men who are utter slaves to stage artistes. And there's no state of slavery more disgraceful than one which is self-imposed. So you needn't allow yourself to be deterred by the snobbish people I've been talking about from showing good humour towards your slaves instead of adopting an attitude of arrogant superiority towards them. Have them respect rather than fear you.
(Robin Campbell, *Seneca: Letters from a Stoic*, Penguin, 1969)

Here in a treatise 'On the Shortness of Life', Seneca discusses how important it is to protect one's time:

Living is the least important activity of the preoccupied man; yet

128

there is nothing which is harder to learn. There are many instruc-
tors in the other arts to be found everywhere: indeed, some of
these arts mere boys have grasped so thoroughly that they can
even teach them. But learning how to live takes a whole life, and,
which may surprise you more, it takes a whole life to learn how
to die. So many of the finest men have put aside all their encum-
brances, renouncing riches and business and pleasure, and made
it their one aim up to the end of their lives to know how to live.
Yet most of these have died confessing that they did not yet know
– still less can those others know. Believe me, it is the sign of a
great man, and one who is above human error, not to allow his
time to be frittered away: he has the longest possible life simply
because whatever time was available he devoted entirely to him-
self. None of it lay fallow and neglected, none of it under
another's control; for being an extremely thrifty guardian of his
time he never found anything for which it was worth exchanging.
So he had enough time; but those into whose lives the public have
made great inroads inevitably have too little.
(C.N.D. Costa, *Seneca: Dialogues and Letters*, Penguin, 1997)

As the leisure age impends, we would do well to listen.

Seneca does not lack dry humour either, closely observing the human
scene to draw some conclusion or other from it. Here he describes the
noises that penetrate the rooms he has taken over the public baths,
which he has done in order to practise ignoring them, forcing his mind
to become self-absorbed:

When the strenuous types are doing their exercises, swinging
weight-laden hands about, I hear the grunting as they toil away –
or go through the motions of toiling away – at them, and the
hissings and strident gasps every time they expel their pent-up
breath ... I hear the smack of a hand pummelling shoulders, then
add someone starting a brawl, and someone else caught thieving,
and the man who likes the sound of his voice in the bath, and the
people who leap into the pool with a tremendous splash ... think
of the hair remover, continually giving vent to his shrill and
penetrating cry in order to advertise his presence, never silent
unless it be while he is plucking someone's armpits and making
the client yell. Then think of the various cries of the man selling

drinks, and the one selling sausages and the other selling pastries, and all the ones hawking for the catering shops.
(Campbell)

At the end of the letter he reports a friend asking him 'Isn't it sometimes a lot simpler just to keep away from the din?' Seneca concedes that it is: 'this is the reason why I shall shortly be moving elsewhere.'

By AD 62 Seneca had had enough of politics, and asked Nero (who by this time was getting seriously out of hand) if he could retire. He was refused, but effectively withdrew from public life. In AD 64 he was implicated in a plot to assassinate Nero and was ordered to commit suicide. His death is recorded in full by the historian Tacitus (*Annals* 15.60ff.), who tells us that even as the blood drained from him, 'his eloquence remained. Summoning his secretaries, he dictated a dissertation.'

It is easy to become slightly sniffy about a rather long-winded, moralising millionaire who guided Nero along the road to power. Yet he never holds himself up as a model, he admits to many of his own failings and has an obvious sympathy for human weakness. Today's millionaires grovelling at the feet of the Labour party do not compare over-favourably.

Seneca ultimately became a figure of very great influence. He was much admired by early Christian writers (though St Augustine thought him a hypocrite). His prose writings were devoured by humanists like Petrarch, Erasmus and Rousseau and his sharp, pointed style had an important effect on the development of English prose in the seventeenth century.

The translations

Watling is his usual readable self; the Hughes' *Oedipus* is a sensational one-off *tour-de-force*. Campbell's selection of letters is judicious and clearly translated, as is Costa's combination of letters and treatises (with an excellent introduction). The Loeb series (Harvard), with facing-page Latin, has the complete works, now somewhat elderly, but still serviceable. Don Share's *Seneca in English* (Penguin, 1998) offers examples of translations of Seneca's poetry (not prose) from the sixteenth century onwards.

18

Martial

It is one of those odd coincidences that there is no Latin poet we know of who was actually born in Rome. But that was where any poet had to come who wanted to succeed in the literary world. Rome was where the wealthy patrons were to back you with their support if you were any good; Rome was where the literary mafia hung out. So there, clutching their styluses, came the budding young writers, from all over Italy and the Roman empire, looking for backers and glory.

Here the brilliant epigrammatist Marcus Valerius Martialis (*c*. AD 40-104), or Martial, born (like Seneca) in Spain, confidently announces himself to this (for him) brave new world:

> He unto whom thou art so partial,
> O reader, is the well-known Martial,
> The epigrammatist: while living,
> Give him the fame thou wouldst be giving
> So shall he hear, and feel and know it:
> Post-obits rarely reach a poet.
> (Lord Byron, in Sullivan and Whigham (eds), *Epigrams of Martial*,
> California, 1987)

Not that patron hunting was much fun – patrons not at home, poor food and drink at their dinners, and much else:

> When, Afer, you returned from Libya home,
> Five time I sought to welcome you to Rome.
> 'He's busy, he sleeps' five times I heard and fled:
> You want no welcome: well, goodbye instead.
> (A. Francis and H. Tatum in J.P. Sullivan and A.J. Boyle (eds),
> *Martial in English*, Penguin, 1996)

131

You drink the best, yet serve us third rate wine.
I'd rather sniff your cup than swill from mine.
(James Michie, *Martial: The Epigrams*, Penguin, 1978)

Cotta will not choose dinner guests, till viewed
Down at the Public Baths, completely nude;
So, since I'm never bidden to a meal,
My private parts must lack some sex-appeal.
(Anthony Reid, in Sullivan and Whigham)

Martial was born at Bilbilis in Spain (near modern Calatayud). He came to Rome in AD 64. There was already a powerful Spanish literary mafia there, including Seneca (the emperor Nero's political adviser), the epic poet Lucan, and the influential professor of education Quintilian. But a failed political conspiracy abruptly ended this coterie (Lucan and Seneca were both instructed to commit suicide – see Chapter 17) and Martial had to begin again. But he eventually made it under Titus (emperor AD 79-81) and Domitian (emperor AD 81-96), and was soon churning out the stuff.

We have in all some twelve volumes of poetry, containing over 1,500 epigrams. Martial knew he was prolific and enjoyed the reputation:

Pudens, you're right: I publish far too much
For my own good. I should emulate my peers
Who squeeze out poetry like precious oils:
One tiny volume every twenty years.
(Richard O'Connell in Sullivan and Boyle)

That there was a price to pay for success – flattery of patrons – was accepted by all Roman poets. Here Martial praises the emperor Domitian's very gripping street-widening policy:

The thrusting shopkeepers had long been poaching
Our city space, front premises encroaching
Everywhere. Then, Domitian, you commanded
That the cramped alleyways should be expanded,
And what were footpaths became real roads.
One doesn't see inn-posts, now, festooned with loads
Of chained flagons; the praetor walks the street

Without the indignity of muddy feet;
Razors aren't wildly waved in people's faces;
Bar-owners, butchers, barbers know their places,
And grimy restaurants can't spill out too far.
Now Rome is Rome, not just a huge bazaar.
(Michie)

If you are going to be nice to your patron, street-widening seems as good a topic as any to wax lyrical about. We may find this cringe-making, but you do not become a good or bad poet simply because you wisely choose to keep your benefactors sweet.

The first point is that Martial was a great poetic innovator. His claim to fame is that, building on Greek epigram and Catullus, he was the first person to turn the epigram into what we (thanks to Martial) expect epigrams to be – clever, sharp, elegant, short poems with a powerful sting in the tail. It is that sting in the tail that counts. Here Martial turns on a critic:

You puff the poets of other days,
    The living you deplore.
Spare me the accolade: your praise
    Is not worth dying for.
(Dudley Fitts in Sullivan and Boyle)

Here the doctor gets it:

I was unwell. You hurried round surrounded
By ninety students, Doctor. Ninety chill,
North-wind-chapped hands then pawed and probed and pounded.
I was unwell: now I'm extremely ill.
(Michie)

Here another doctor is pasted:

Doctor Diaulus has changed his trade:
He now is a mortician,
With the same results he got before
As a practising physician.
(Dorothy Wender in Sullivan and Boyle)

18. Martial

Here his chum Gallicus is told the truth:

> 'Please, Marcus, tell the truth,' you say,
> 'That's all I want to hear!'
> If you read a poem or plead a case
> You din it in my ear:
> 'The truth, the honest truth!' you beg,
> It's damned hard to deny
> Such a request. So here's the truth:
> *You'd rather have me lie.*
> (Wender in Sullivan and Boyle)

A fellow litterateur is put in his place:

> Why don't I send you my little books, Pontilianus?
> For fear you might send me yours, Pontilianus.
> (D.R. Shackleton Bailey, *Martial: Epigrams vol. II*, Loeb Classical
> Library no. 95, Harvard, 1993)

The second point is that Martial's view was panoramic. Here was real life – contemporary people of all social backgrounds and their personal customs, habits and practices – put under his sharp, unforgiving microscope to be revealed, warts and all, in exquisitely clever verse: the kaleidoscope of Rome in miniature, high art. The sheer range of Martial's coverage within so restricted a medium broke new poetic ground.

Here are some sexy topics:

> Marulla's hobby is to measure
> Erections. These she weighs at leisure
> By hand and afterwards announces
> Her estimate in pounds and ounces.
> Once it's performed its exercise
> And done its job and your cock lies
> Rag-limp, again she'll calculate,
> Manually, the loss in weight.
> Hand? It's a grocer's balance-plate!
> (Michie)

Fabullus, do you want to know why Mister
Themison has no wife? He has his sister.
(Jim Powell, in Sullivan and Whigham)

Lewd dinner hosts keep asking you back.
Are you the entrée or the midnight snack?
(Philip Murray, in Sullivan and Boyle)

Martial can be very abusive:

When Galla for her health goeth to the Bathe,
She carefully doth hide, as is most meete,
With aprons of fine linnen, or a sheete,
Those parts, that modesty concealed hath:
Nor onely those, but e'en the brest and necke,
That might be seene, or showne, without all checke.
But yet one foule, and unbeseeming place
She leaves uncovered still: What's that? Her face.
(Sir John Harington in Sullivan and Boyle)

Here Martial attends a slave-auction:

Last week, the auctioneer was trying to sell
A girl whose reputation one could smell
From here to her street corner in the slums.
After some time, when only paltry sums
Were being offered, wishing to assure
The crowd that she was absolutely pure,
He pulled the unwilling 'lot' across and smacked
Three or four kisses on her. Did this act
Make any difference to the price? It did.
The highest offerer withdrew his bid.
(Michie)

But Martial is not all biting satire and wit. Here he also shows himself master of the epitaph, as with wonderful tenderness he commends a beloved slave-girl who died young to the care of his own dead parents down in Hades:

18. Martial

To you, my parents, I send on
This little girl Erotion,
The slave I loved, that by your side
Her ghost need not be terrified
Of the pitch darkness underground
Or the great jaws of Hades' hound.
This winter she would have completed
Her sixth year had she not been cheated
By just six days. Lisping my name
May she continue the sweet game
Of childhood happily down there
In two such good, old spirits' care.
Lie lightly on her, turf and dew:
She put so little weight on you.
(Michie)

Martial did not see out his time in Rome. When Domitian died in AD 96 the new regime was not sympathetic to him, and in AD 98 he returned to Spain, where he died, still writing.

The translations

Given the demands made by a miniaturist like Martial, the overall standard is remarkably high. Michie provides facing Latin text (as does Gould in the new Loeb series); Sullivan/Whigham (also with Latin) and Sullivan/Boyle make excellent selections of translations from down the ages.

19

Tacitus

Had the greatest of Latin historians Tacitus been alive today, he would have made a brilliant presenter of late-night political TV: crisp, punchy, master of the innuendo, the one-liner and teasingly suggestive question, hard-bitten, cynical, and always on the look-out for weaknesses.

Here is Tacitus in wham-bang style, wondering whether the two armies fighting it out for supremacy in the civil war between Otho and Vitellius (AD 69) might have laid down their arms and let the Senate take over, as one Paulinus suggested:

> I am quite prepared to grant that in their heart of hearts a few men may have prayed for peace in preference to strife and for a good and honest ruler instead of two worthless and infamous scoundrels. Yet in an age and society so degenerate, I do not believe that the prudent Paulinus expected the ordinary soldier to exercise such self-control as to lay down their arms from an attachment to peace, after disturbing the peace from love of war. Nor do I think that ... officers and generals whose consciences were in most cases burdened with the recollection of a life of pleasure, bankruptcy and crime would have tolerated as emperor any other than a disreputable character from whom they could demand payment for the services they had rendered.
> (K. Wellesley, *Tacitus: The Histories*, Penguin, 1975)

Ouch.

Publius Cornelius Tacitus (AD 56-c.120) wrote history covering the period AD 14-96 – the early emperors of Rome (though not all of his work survives). And he knew what he was talking about. He was a political animal through and through. He served in various capacities under the emperors Vespasian, Titus and Domitian (AD 69-96) and was proconsul in Asia AD 112-13. So he knew the system backwards – and did not like what he saw of it. Of the period when he was in politics, he says:

> The government imagined it could silence the voice of Rome and annihilate the freedom of the Senate and men's knowledge of the truth ... We have indeed set up a record of subservience. Rome of old explored the utmost limits of freedom; we have plumbed the depths of slavery, robbed as we are by informers even of the right to exchange ideas in conversation. We should have lost our memories as well as our tongues had it been as easy to forget as to be silent.
> (H. Mattingley, rev. S. Handford, *Tacitus on Britain and Germany*, Penguin, 1970)

So there is real passion about Tacitus' work. He wanted to set the record straight. He is sensitive, however, that this may not make the most gripping reading. Here he does what no author ever does and actually *apologises* for the unattractiveness of his history, because there is such a dearth of fine examples and stirring events in the period he is describing:

> What interests and stimulates readers is a geographical description, the changing fortune of a battle, the glorious death of a commander. My themes on the other hand concern cruel orders, unremitting accusations, treacherous friendships, innocent men ruined – a conspicuously monotonous glut of downfalls and their monotonous causes.
> (Michael Grant, *Tacitus: The Annals of Imperial Rome*, Penguin, 1996)

Nevertheless, he goes on, there is method in this apparent madness:

> Now that Rome has virtually been transformed into an autocracy, the investigation and record of these details concerning the autocrat may prove useful. Indeed, it is from such studies – from the experience of others – that most men learn to distinguish right and wrong, advantage and disadvantage. Few can tell them apart instinctively.
> (Grant)

History, in other words, as for all ancient historians, has a high moral purpose.

Here Tacitus analyses when the autocratic rot set in. It was, he reckoned, with Augustus (first emperor, 31 BC-AD 14), who came to sole power after years of civil war (see Chapter 15 on Virgil). Read it carefully. This is typical Tacitus:

> Augustus found the whole state exhausted by internal dissensions and established over it a personal regime known as the principate ... he seduced the army with bonuses, and his cheap food policy was successful bait for civilians. Indeed, he attracted everybody's good-will by the enjoyable gift of peace. Then he gradually pushed ahead and absorbed the function of the senate, the officials and even the law. Opposition did not exist. War or judicial murder had disposed of all men of spirit.
> (Grant)

The point is that nothing in this brief analysis is historically wrong, but the tone is utterly negative. Is this just? What one must do is observe how Tacitus frames the argument. Observe:

- how good points are buried under bad points. One of Augustus' great achievements was to restore peace after the terrible years of civil war, but this is lost in accusations of bribery and of autocratic designs on the constitution.
- how innocent actions are given the worst possible gloss. Augustus' cheap food policy was standard Roman practice and there is no evidence to suggest that he was any more lavish than anyone else.
- how damaging innuendo is allowed to stand. Thus 'war and judicial murder had disposed of all men of spirit' raises the questions – war waged by whom, and why? And murder by whom? The innuendo is that all this war and murder was Augustus' sole responsibility.

You can see why Tacitus would have been a star turn on TV.

Alongside this subtle organising of material to undermine what may be wholly innocent, Tacitus is always insinuating motives for action. Here Sejanus, an increasingly powerful and hated adviser to Tiberius (second emperor, AD 14-37), is worried that Tiberius is losing faith in him:

So he set about persuading Tiberius to consider enjoying life in some beautiful place far from Rome. The advantages of this course were numerous: Sejanus would control physical access to Tiberius, and would for the most control approaches to him by using letters, conveyed by soldiers of the Praetorian Guard. Tiberius, he thought, under the influences of advancing age and the pleasures of privacy, would be more ready to hand over to him some responsibility for government. In any case he would stand less risk of unpopularity if he shed his crowd of visitors [*i.e. people trying to suck up to Tiberius and, by implication, Sejanus*], and by removing the trappings, his real power would be increased. So over a period he persuaded Tiberius of the aggravations of city life, with its masses of people and visitors. He extolled the merits of peace and quiet where the emperor would not have to endure things that bored and upset him, and where he could give full attention to the things that really mattered.

(D. Shotter, *Tacitus: Annals IV*, Aris and Phillips, 1989)

And so Tiberius is bundled off to Capri, leaving Sejanus pulling the strings back in Rome. One can imagine Tacitus on TV asking Peter Mandelson about Prime Minister Blair's lengthy holidays with his rich chums in Tuscany with similar innuendo. True or not, the easy credibility of Tacitus' suggested motives for Sejanus' actions leaves an indelible impression.

The point is that Tacitus is a master of persuasion. No device escapes him. So it is not surprising that he is also a master of human psychology – for successful persuaders have to know what makes people tick. This was largely down to the Roman educational system which, in its advanced stages, was designed to serve the wealthy and turn them into politicians and public servants. Since the ability to persuade was as much the key to advancement in the Roman as in the modern world, techniques of persuasion and learning how to argue a case had a central place in the education system. The Romans called this 'rhetoric'. We call it 'communication skills'.

Tacitus had learned these lessons well. Here he imagines how Calgacus, the British leader attempting to stem the Roman advance into Scotland in AD 83, might have addressed his men on the subject of Romans:

'Robbers of the world, now that earth fails their all-devastating hands, they probe even the sea; if their enemy has wealth, they have greed; if he be poor, they are ambitious; East nor West has glutted them; alone of mankind they covet with the same passion want as much as wealth. To plunder, butcher, steal, these things they misname empire; they make a desolation and they call it peace. Children and kin are by the law of nature each man's dearest possessions; they are swept away from us by conscription to be slaves in other lands; our wives and sisters, even when they escape a soldier's lust, are debauched by self-styled friends and guests: our goods and chattels go for tribute; our lands and harvests in requisition of grain.'
(*Tacitus vol. I*, Loeb Classical Library no. 35, Heinemann-Harvard, 1970)

What an indictment, too, of Rome!

Here, fascinated as he was by crowd psychology, Tacitus describes part of the battle for Rome in which the emperor Vitellius was deposed in AD 69:

The people came and watched the fighting, cheering and applauding now one side, now the other, like spectators at a gladiatorial contest. Whenever one side gave ground, and the soldiers hid in shops or sought refuge in some private house, they clamoured for them to be dragged out and slaughtered. In this way they got the greater part of the plunder for themselves: for while the soldiers were busy with the bloody work of massacre, the spoil fell to the crowd.

The scene throughout the city was cruel and distorted: on the one side fighting and wounded men, on the other baths and restaurants; here lay heaps of bleeding dead, and close at hands were harlots and their ilk. All the vice and licence of luxurious peace, and all the crime and horror of a captured town. You would have thought the city mad with fury and riotous with pleasure at the same time.
(D.S. Levene, *Tacitus: The Histories*, World's Classics, 1997)

Tacitus claims to have written 'without anger and prejudice'. My aunt Fanny. But what a journalist!

19. Tacitus

The translations

Tacitus' brilliantly lethal, pointed, concise prose style, stabbing like a legionary's short sword, is irreproduceable in English. All the translations are readable and engaging, with useful introductions and indices (Levene has very good notes too). Shotter has facing-page Latin and commentary on the English; the Loeb has facing-page Latin.

20

Juvenal

It is anger that drives the satirist, and the greatest of Roman satirists, Juvenal (*c.* AD 60-130), whipped himself up into frantic paddies more often than most. Here in the first of his sixteen satires that have come down to us he gives a taste of his feelings about contemporary Rome:

> No Age can go beyond us: Future Times
> Can add no farther to the present Crimes.
> Our sons but the same things can wish and do;
> Vice is at stand, and at the highest flow.
> Then Satyr, spread thy Sails: take all the winds can blow.
> (John Dryden in A. Poole and J. Maule (eds), *The Oxford Book of Classical Verse in Translation*, Oxford, 1995)

Juvenal is here staking a claim to the high moral ground. He must make it look as if he is a man of decency forced into writing, not out of spite but out of virtuous necessity.

Buoyed, then, by indignant self-righteousness, Juvenal launches out to flay the city of Rome, the court of the emperors, women, the upper classes, sexual deviants, the rich, the greedy, everyone who has, in his view, betrayed what it means to be a true Roman.

In Satire 3 he pictures a true-blue Roman complaining about the city – full of corrupt foreigners (Greeks) and Flash Harrys with more money than sense, and impossible to live in for the traffic, noise, crowds, tottering tenements and thugs. Here he pictures the street bully carefully avoiding the aristocrat with a bodyguard, but:

> ... for me, a lonely pedestrian, trudging home by moonlight
> or with hand cupped round the wick of one poor guttering candle,
> he has only contempt. Hear how this wretched quarrel starts
> (a *quarrel*? when you're the fighter and I'm just the punchbag?):

144

he blocks my way, tells me to stop. I have to obey him –
what else can you do when attacked by a raging tough who's
stronger
than you are? 'Where have you sprung from?' he shouts ...
... 'Nothing to say? Speak up or I'll kick your teeth in!
Tell me, where's your pitch? What synagogue do you doss in?'
Whether you try to answer or back away in silence
makes no odds, you're beaten up anyway – then your irate 'victim'
takes *you* to court! Such, then, is the poor man's 'freedom':
After being slugged to a pulp, he may beg for his last few
remaining teeth to be left him, as a special favour
(Peter Green, *Juvenal: The Sixteen Satires*, Penguin, 1998)

It all rings a bell today – especially the lines about the prosecution of the victim.

Then there are the powerful. Here in Satire 4 Juvenal describes a humble fisherman terrified at the thought of what might happen to him if he tries to sell a turbot he has caught, so big that 'every Inspector of Seaweed for miles around would pounce on this wretched boatman, all quoting law, to wit, that the fish had strayed from Caesar's imperial ponds'. So he decides to present it as a gift to the emperor Domitian. He travels overland with it and finally reaches the royal palace:

The wondering crowd, that gathered to survey
The enormous fish and bar the fisher's way,
Satiate at length retires; the gates unfold;
Murmuring the excluded senators behold
The envied dainty enter. On the man
To 'great Atrides' [*Agamemnon, i.e. the emperor*] pressed and thus
    began:
'This, for a private table far too great,
Accept. The day as festive celebrate.
Make haste to load your stomach and devour
A turbot destined for this happy hour.
I sought him not: he marked the toils I set,
And rushed, a willing victim, to my net.'
Was flattery e'er so rank? Yet He grows vain,
And his crest rises at the fulsome strain.
When to divine a mortal power we raise,

He credits all hyperbole of praise.
(W. Gifford and S. Braund, *Juvenal: Satires, with the Satires of Persius*, Everyman, 1992)

This is a superb parody of procedure at the emperor's court, and all for a turbot – the admiring crowds, the ritual entrance (the senators are kept outside while the fish enters), the humble fisherman's grand language, the picture of the turbot keenly rushing into the net for the privilege of being presented to Domitian. But this is what you can expect when the emperor is an unpredictable tyrant, in a court where, as Juvenal goes on to say, 'men's throats are cut with a whisper'.

Women too attract Juvenal's scorn. In Satire 6, the longest satire in Roman literature, Juvenal advises a friend about to marry (don't – you're better off committing suicide, or with a pretty boy), and goes on to list the vices of today's upper-class married women. It is a familiar litany: they're sex-mad, faithless, spendthrift, loud-mouthed, vain, trivial, blue-stockings, murderous, too keen to assume men's roles, not interested in babies, and so on. Here is Messalina, wife of the emperor Claudius, mother of Britannicus, disguised with a red wig and the name of Lycisca, in a brothel:

> Th'Imperiall Strumpet with one Maid, stole out
> In her night-hoods, and having cast about
> Her black hair, a red periwigge; she got
> Into the Stewes, where th'old rugge still was hot;
> Had a spare room, kept for her. There gold-chained,
> Bare-breasted stood, her name Lycisca fained;
> High borne Britannicus, thy womb displayed;
> Smil'd upon all that came, her bargaine made.
> And when the Wenches were dismis'd, she last,
> ('Twas all she could) sadly the door made fast,
> And many thirsted-for encounters tried,
> Departed tir'd with men, not satisfy'd,
> And foul'd with candle-smoak, her cheeks smear'd o'er,
> The Brothell-steame she to her pillow bore.
> (Sir Robert Stapylton, in Poole and Maule)

All very disgusting. But that is the point. A satirist is not interested in balance or fairness, let alone political correctness (as if there had been

such a thing at Rome). He identifies a victim, trains all his armoury on it and lets fly. Nevertheless, there is a special problem with Juvenal in this respect – as he says, his satire is directed not at the living but at the dead. None of his targets was alive when he was writing. What did he mean by this? That the whole system was so corrupt that it did not *matter* whom you attacked, since the moral would be understood anyway (and the wise satirist protects his back)? Or was it that he was merely a tool of the current emperors, attacking past régimes to make the present appear all the more lustrous?

But if one aspect of the satirist is the attack on folly, the other is the defence of righteousness. A satirist must appear to be a man of positive principle, or his authority disappears. It is in Juvenal's more ironic and cynical later satires, where he does not lay into individuals so much as reflect on human situations and characteristics, that this moralising tendency comes to the fore.

In Satire 10, nick-named 'The Vanity of Human Wishes' by Dr Johnson in 1749 who imitated it, Juvenal reflects on how futile human aspirations are. Even prayer itself is a waste of time. Byron thought it should be read to all the dying in preference to Church services. Juvenal goes on:

> Is there nothing, then, that people should pray for? If you want
>   some advice,
> You will let the heavenly powers themselves determine what blessings
> Are most appropriate to us and best suit our conditions;
> For instead of what's pleasant, the gods will always provide what's
>   fitting.
> They care more for man than he cares for himself; for we
> Are driven by the force of emotion, a blind overmastering impulse,
> When we yearn for marriage and a wife who will give us children;
>   the gods,
> However, foresee what the wife and children are going to be like.
> Still, that you may have something to ask for – some reason to offer
> The holy sausages and innards of a little white pig in a chapel –
> You ought to pray for a healthy mind in a healthy body.
> Ask for a valiant heart which has banished the fear of death,
> Which looks upon length of days as one of the least of nature's Gifts …
> The things that I recommend you can grant to yourself; it is certain
> That the tranquil life can only be reached by the path of goodness.

20. Juvenal

Lady Luck, if the truth were known, you possess no power;
It is we who make you a goddess and give you a place in heaven.
(Niall Rudd, *Juvenal: The Satires*, World's Classics, 1991)

Juvenal invented satire. Today it is a booming industry, and it hasn't changed much. Satirists still embrace the same sorts of attitudes (an impossibly corrupt present set against a golden past, an age of innocence) and attack the same sorts of targets (individuals and fads, but never the system that produces them), with as little success in fomenting change (as if mere laughter could achieve that).

Were he still alive, Juvenal would be moaning that he didn't take out the copyright.

The translations

Like Tacitus, Juvenal's deadly thrusts are almost impossible to catch in modern English. Green generally catches the tone well; Rudd is much more accurate without losing readability, but less sharp; Gifford's more antiquated style has its virtues, but tends to gloss over the filth. Poole and Maule cover all Classical literature with translations from every age.

Index

Main chapters are indicated in italics, e.g. *31-40*.
All of the lesser-known names from personal poetry and epigram are
included.

Index

Epic: nature of 7; as tragedy 7; subject-matter 23

Epicurus: and Lucretius 101

Epigrams, Greek: *85-90*; as inscriptions 85; as literature 86; death 86-7; sex 87-9; satire 89-90; pessimism 90; and Catullus 105-6; and Martial 134

Euripides: *60-8*; and Aristophanes 60; and Aristotle 60-1; psychology 61-2; and women 61-2; melodramatic 64-6; 'modern' 66

First World War: and Homer 4

Folk-tale: and oral poetry 13; and lyric poetry 29

Gods: as forces 1; indifferent to humans 13, 100; support favourites 13, 45; less evident in *Odyssey* 17; and justice 17; and Odysseus 18; in epic and tragedy 43-4; in Herodotus 52; excluded in Thucydides 56; ruthlessness in *Bacchae* 66; discounted by philosophers 76; in Virgil 114

Greeks: values as shown in Homer 22; attitude to poetry 23; and Roman literature 85, 92

Hector: death foreseen 9; sympathetic 10; death 11

Hellenistic age: 86

Heraclitus: 76

Herodotus: on crocodiles and ants 3; *47-53*; on Trojan War 47; questioning the past 48; wide sympathies 48; praises Egypt 50; 'father of lies' 50; structure of history 51-2; organising principle 51-2; rational 52; divine background to 52; compared with Thucydides 56

Hipponax: 25

History: and Herodotus 47-53; history before Herodotus 47-8; see also Thucydides and Tacitus

Homer: *Iliad 7-14*; reticence 11; similes 12-13; gods 13-14; attitudes of heroes to gods 13; no theology 14; as oral poetry 14, 15; *Odyssey 15-22*; *Odyssey* as folk-tale; structure of *Odyssey* 15-16; gods in

Odyssey 17-18; as first and best 20-1; Homeric man and Greeks 22; location 29; and Virgil 113-14, 118

Howerd, Frankie: and Roman comedy 91

Ibycus: 27-8

Iliad: see Homer

Juvenal: and *Private Eye* 3; *144-9*; anger and self-righteousness 144; emperors 145-6; women 146; purpose 147-8; invents satire 149

Leonidas: 87

Lesbia: see Catullus

Literature: western 1; Roman and Greek 85, 92; political links 126; and personal feeling 23, 126; and patronage 131

Love: and lyric poets 27-8; in Ovid 119-20

Lucilius: 89-90

Lucretius: on death 2, 99; *99-104*; religion as evil 99-100; gods indifferent 100; soul does not survive death 101; Epicurus 101; content of poem 101-2; ethics 102; imagery 102-4

Lyric poetry: *23-30*; public performance 23; survival of 23-4

Maecenas: Augustus' minister of culture 112, 126

Marcus Aurelius: on death 4

Martial: *131-7*; born in Spain 131-2; and patronage 131-2; and Seneca 132; praise of emperors 132; inventor of epigram 134; range 135; tenderness 136-7; death 137

Meleager: 87-8

Menander: and Plautus 92-6; and Byron 96

Mime: as popular drama 75

Music: and poetic performance 23, 31, 32

Nero: and Seneca 126

Odysseus: and Athene 18; much-enduring 18; intelligent 19; contrast with Achilles 20; and Virgil 113

Odyssey: see Homer

Oedipus: in Aeschylus 31; in Sophocles 43

Index